# WHO KNEW?

# WHO KNEW?

## FORMULAS AND SOLUTIONS FOR A NATURALLY CLEAN HOME

**JEANNE BOSSOLINA LUBIN
AND
BRUCE LUBIN**

**Castle Point
Publishing**

Castle Point Publishing
Hoboken, NJ

## DEDICATION

To Jack, Terrence, and Aidan, as always.

## ACKNOWLEDGMENTS

We're indebted to our families for putting up with sprays, smells, and science experiments we conducted in the process of creating this book, and for never judging us as we came close to burning down the house in the pursuit of the perfect green solutions. James Tavendale has been an invaluable go-to guy, and an all around good dude to boot. Joy Mangano continues to amaze us with her energy, sound advice, and big brain, and we're tremendously grateful to be part of her team. Finally, special thanks to Brian Scevola, who deals with us every day and, incredibly, hasn't developed an ulcer or dependency problem. We couldn't pull this off without you, Brian.

# CONTENTS

**CHAPTER 1**
INTRODUCTION

8

**CHAPTER 2**
KITCHEN

18

**CHAPTER 3**
CARPET STAIN REMOVAL

46

**CHAPTER 4**
LIVING AREAS

58

**CHAPTER 5**
BATHROOM

82

**CHAPTER 6**
BEDROOM

102

**CHAPTER 7**
WINDOWS & OUTSIDE SPACES 110

**CHAPTER 8**
CLOTHING STAINS 124

**CHAPTER 9**
LAUNDRY 150

**CHAPTER 10**
METALS & JEWELRY 164

**CHAPTER 11**
HEALTH & BEAUTY 174

**CHAPTER 12**
BABIES & PETS 200

**CHAPTER 13**
PEST CONTROL 210

# 1

# INTRODUCTION

*Who Knew? Formulas and Solutions for a Naturally Clean Home* aims to help you avoid chemicals, reducing indoor pollution levels, and instead use natural products to keep your house clean inside and out.

Just because something is a natural product does not mean it is not dangerous. For example, the naturally occurring mineral salt borax is an excellent stain remover and has numerous uses around the home. However, it is *poisonous* and it can make the skin peel and itch, so do not use around children or pets, and wear gloves when using. Keep all cleaning products stored safely.

There are many benefits from using the natural cleaning solutions given in this book. Not only will you be reducing exposure to toxins of everyone in your home (and especially the person doing the cleaning) but also you will be contributing less to the chemicals released into the environment. Packaging will be less and you will also save money because commercially produced cleaning products usually cost more than these homemade versions, which can be just as effective.

There are a lot of tips and solutions in this book so if you are used to using chemical products in your home, start simple and progress slowly. Below is a list of the main ingredients you will need for the solutions given in this book.

1. BAKING SODA
2. BORAX
3. CLUB SODA
4. CREAM OF TARTAR
5. ESSENTIAL OILS
6. GLYCERIN
7. LEMONS
8. NATURAL DISHWASHING LIQUID SOAP
9. PURE OR CASTILE SOAP
10. SALT
11. WASHING SODA
12. DISTILLED WHITE VINEGAR

# GETTING STARTED: YOUR TOP TWELVE

You probably have many of the items listed below already—what kitchen doesn't have baking soda, salt, vinegar and lemons? Make a point of stocking the other items, however, and you're one the way to a naturally clean home!

**BAKING SODA** is mildly alkaline and effective at neutralizing mild acids. It is a terrific—and inexpensive—cleaner, deodorizer, and stain remover. It can be used to:

- clean burnt food at the bottom of pots and pans (pg. 28)
- whiten old linen (pg. 154)
- brighten old silver (pg. 169)
- eliminate old ink stains from fabric and carpets (pg. 53)

**BORAX** forms an alkaline antiseptic solution when dissolved in water and is effective as a disinfectant, water softener, and detergent. Borax is also great for loosening grease and dirt, so it's a valuable stain remover. Use it to:

- loosen grease and dirt, and remove stubborn stains when mixed with glycerin and liquid castile soap (pg. 153)
- sponge away syrup stains in carpet and fabric (pg. 56)
- clean the bathroom when mixed with baking soda (pg. 93)

**CLUB SODA** can be used to:
- immediately treat fresh stains on fabric and carpets (pg. 48)
- clean windows (pg. 112)
- remove stains from clothes when in a restaurant (pg. 143)

**CREAM OF TARTAR** is a mildly acidic powder which, when combined with baking soda, forms baking powder. It's effective for:
- cleaning the rings around shirt collars (pg. 131)
- attacking stubborn stains (pg. 128)

**ESSENTIAL OILS** can be used to:
- scent cleaning and bath products (pg. 84)
- remove adhesive labels (pg. 67)
- give a dark bathtub a great shine (pg. 93)
- treat bloodstains on both fabric and carpet (pg. 49)

**GLYCERIN** is a syrupy, odorless liquid commonly used in cake frosting to keep it from hardening. In cleaning, though, it's effective at loosening stubborn stains, and can be used to:
- lift chocolate stains out of the carpet (pg. 50)
- remove newsprint stains (pg. 140)
- get rid of perfume stains that linger in fabric or carpets (pg. 141)
- help remove tough laundry stains when used as a presoak (pg. 156)

# WHAT ARE ESSENTIAL OILS?

Essential oils are non-toxic, highly concentrated oils derived from aromatic plants or herbs, which are the basis of many of the cleaning formulas described in this book. When used properly, they offer wonderful aromas and can rid your house of mold, odors, viruses, and more. You can choose from many varieties, and they give your home a lovely, unique scent. Essential oils are available in health food stores, mail order catalogs, and on many Internet sites.

When buying essential oils, make sure they are undiluted and not mixed with carrier oil. (Typically, when essential oils are mixed that way it is to create aromatherapy oil, which is used for massage, not cleaning.) Store your essential oils away from light, and they will last indefinitely. You can chose any scent you like—here are our suggestions for your essential oils you might want to get started with:

- tea tree
- lemon or orange
- rosemary
- peppermint

- lavender
- basil
- thyme
- eucalyptus

With these oils, you can virtually clean and deodorize your entire home, rid your home of pests, and scent your bedroom, kitchen, bathroom, and laundry beautifully!

Many of the formulas in this book suggest combinations of essential oils. However, you can experiment at home, and find the fragrances you like best. Here are some of our favorite combinations:

**LEMON** is commonly known as "nature's bleach." It's a great cleaning agent, particularly when mixed with baking soda. Use lemon juice to:

- clean away stains on many metals (pg. 166)
- remove rust stains from fabric (pg. 144)
- get rid of tea stains (pg. 147)

**NATURAL DISHWASHING LIQUID SOAP** is available in supermarkets nationwide and can be used to:

- clean windows (pg. 112)
- make your own surface cleaners (pg. 33)
- clean bamboo and willow (pg. 71)
- make carpet shampoo (pg. 65)

**CASTILE SOAP** is a pure soap that can be bought in health food stores either as a solid or as a liquid. It's a mild soap made of olive and coconut oils, so it is great if you have dry skin. In addition, castile contains no synthetic detergents or animal fats, and it's completely biodegradable. Use it to:

- pre-treat laundry before washing (pg. 159)
- make a laundry powder for lace (pg. 160)
- wash delicate clothing such as lingerie (pg. 156)

**SALT** is prized as a cleaner for its abrasive actions, and is most effective when combined with lemon juice. Use salt to:

- remove stains gently from bone cutlery handles (pg. 39)
- clean egg-stained fabric (pg. 132)
- clean away soap build-up from glass shower curtains (pg. 89)
- clean up food spills in the oven (pg. 24)

**WASHING SODA** is an inexpensive, crystalline powder that is a main ingredient in the laundry detergents sold today. Use it to:

- make up laundry powders or liquids that will clean your clothes naturally and work well in hard water areas (pg. 159)
- reduce calcium deposits in the washing machine and reduce the amount of washing powder needed (pg. 154)
- clean stone floors (pg. 66)
- unblock drains (pg. 96)

**WHITE VINEGAR** is perhaps the one ingredient you cannot live without! Not only is it effective for cleaning thousands of household items, it also is a disinfectant, fights mold, and deodorizes, too. Use it to:

- treat yellow stains on white clothes (pg. 149)
- remove alcohol stains from fabric (pg. 127)
- clean away paint spots on windows and mirrors (pg. 114)
- clean and sanitize the bathroom (pg. 94)

**OTHER USEFUL ITEMS** to have in your home are:

- small jars: for mixing up paste for spot cleaning

- shakers: for jobs that require shaking out a powder cleaner (you can punch holes in the lid of any suitable container to make a shaker)

- large plastic containers: refill with your own homemade versions to reuse the containers (re-use your old non-organic laundry detergent ones)

- spray bottles: the 16 fl oz. sized ones are good (again, you may already have these from commercial cleaners)

- a nest of cups: for measuring out ¼ of a cup, ½ a cup, 1 full cup etc. (you may already have these for baking)

- a funnel: if you are going to be making up formulas in bottles with narrow necks such as spray bottles

- spoons: a teaspoon and a tablespoon

- a dropper for each essential oil, unless the bottle has the capacity to "pour" a drop at a time

Cleaning can play havoc with your nails, so protect them by running your nails over a bar of soap to stop debris from getting underneath. Wear rubber gloves when dipping your hands into hot water or using cleaning products, otherwise they will redden and become dry. Moisturize well afterwards.

When using new cleaning products or techniques, experiment with a small, inconspicuous area first so you know whether the object is colorfast or the cleaning method likely to cause damage. In addition, it's important to follow the rules below when treating any stains.

# 2.

# KITCHEN

Your kitchen is where the family congregates, and where guests linger as well. In their wake, they sometimes leave dirt and debris, right? Of course, the kitchen is also where all your chopping, pouring, and cooking takes place—meaning it has the potential to be the dirtiest room in your home! If you follow these tips, though, your kitchen will sparkle—naturally and inexpensively.

# VINEGAR, THE NATURAL GREASE CUTTER

Ah, vinegar, is there anything it *can't* clean? When you've got extra greasy dishes, just add a little vinegar (and lemon juice) to your dishwasher and watch your dishes sparkle.

## HOMEMADE DISHWASHING LIQUID

Make your own dishwashing liquid by mixing 4 fl oz. of unscented natural dishwashing soap with 10 drops each of lemon and orange oils. Shake well as use instead of your normal dishwashing liquid.

## APPLE RINSE

A wonderful rinse for your glasses can be made if you mix 8 fl oz. of apple cider vinegar with 20 drops each of lemon and orange oils. Add 2 tablespoons of the liquid to a sink full of clean water when rinsing glassware, and store the rest of your formula for future use.

## REACH FOR THE PLUNGER AND THE PETROLEUM JELLY

If you have a stopped drain, use a rubber plunger over the uncovered drain. Plungers work by creating pressure to clear the blockage so make sure you have the drain completely covered. Block the overflow with a wet rag if required. Make sure the seal is tight, using petroleum jelly on the rim of the plunger if needed. Push and pull several times before pulling the plunger up on the last go.

## THE NATURAL WAY TO UNBLOCK DRAINS

To unblock drains without resorting to harsh drain cleaners try this simple formula.

½ cup washing powder or baking soda

½ cup distilled white vinegar

½ cup salt

boiling water

Pour the either washing soda or baking soda down the drain, followed by the distilled white vinegar. Leave it for an hour or so to do its work, then pour in the salt and 5 or 6 cups of boiling water.

## THE SNAKE SOLUTION

Use a plumber's snake for clogged drains before you reach for the abrasive chemicals. The acids in them are better kept out of our wastewater. To work through standing water, pour in 1 cup of washing soda first, wait for it to settle, then trying the baking soda technique above.

# IT'S EASY TO PREVENT BLOCKED DRAINS...

...Just make sure you never pour grease down the kitchen drain and you'll probably never have a clogged drain. It's important to always use a cover or strainer to stop food going down the drain and blocking the pipes, too.

# TO CLEAN YOUR DISHWASHER

To brighten up a dull dishwasher, run the machine empty on a short cycle with 2 cups of vinegar in the detergent receptacle. You can use a toothpick to remove any food particles trapped in the spray arm.

## SIMPLY SPARKLING STAINLESS STEEL SINKS (SAY THAT THREE TIMES FAST)

Stainless steel sinks can lose their luster and appear dull. This mix will bring back its natural shine: Sprinkle 2 tablespoons of baking soda and 2 tablespoons of salt in the sink covering as much surface area as you can, and scrub with a suitable scourer. Make sure to get into all the hard-to-reach places. Then rinse with hot water and give it a final wipe with a cloth dipped in distilled white vinegar.

## MAKE YOUR OWN DISHWASHER POWDER— IT'S CHEAP AND IT'S GREEN

You can make homemade, phosphate-free dishwasher soap with this simple formula: Just mix 1 tablespoon of borax, 3 tablespoons of baking soda, and 2 drops of lemon oil. Use this mix in your dishwasher after rinsing all food off the dishes. You'll never use store-bought again.

## YELLOW SPOTS ON YOUR DISHES?

Sorry to hear about it. If your dishes have yellow spots after emerging from the dishwasher, just run it, empty, with a package of lemonade mix in the soap holder. It really does the trick.

## GET RID OF THAT FUNKY GARBAGE DISPOSAL SMELL, PART I

Kitchen garbage disposal units can contain bacteria and emit unpleasant odors. Mix together ¼ cup of borax, ¼ cup of baking soda, and the rind of half a lemon. Pour the mixture down into the disposal unit and turn it on, using plenty of hot water, and the smell will disappear.

## GET RID OF THAT FUNKY GARBAGE DISPOSAL SMELL, PART II

Another idea to get rid of grease and create a pleasant smell at the same time is to drop 3 ice cubes of frozen vinegar and a few pieces of citrus peel down your disposal and grind them up. It will be noisy but will give off a citrus fragrance.

# NO ONE HOME?

If you are going away for a few days, make sure food waste that could start to smell is not left in the disposal unit. To flush away any remains, plug the sink, fill with around 2 inches of water and run the disposer while the water drains.

## Who Knew?

Over 47% of all homes in the United States have garbage disposal units.

# ACRYLIC SINKS

Never use an abrasive cleanser or scourer on acrylic sinks or you risk scratches. Watermarks can be removed from an acrylic sink with distilled white vinegar on a damp cloth.

## DIRTY DISHES

A great idea if you are not going to wash dirty dishes right away is to keep some baking soda in a shaker in your kitchen. Scrape food off the plates and then sprinkle with the baking soda. This will get to work right away and it won't matter if you don't wash dishes for a few hours or even overnight. No rinsing is needed and you can load the dishes into the dishwasher or sink as they are.

## CHROME IN THE KITCHEN

Restore luster to chrome trim on taps and kitchen appliances by polishing with baby oil and a soft cloth. You can remove any rust spots with crumpled-up aluminum foil.

## OVEN SMARTS

When cleaning your oven, swiftness saves the day. As soon as a spill occurs, immediately cover it with salt. When the oven has cooled, brush away the burnt-on food with a damp sponge. You'll find most of the spill is gone.

## TWO SIMPLE WAYS TO CLEAN YOUR OVEN

To keep you oven clean without toxic oven cleaners, once every few weeks just sprinkle baking soda on a clean damp cloth and wipe over the inside of the oven and the door. To clean up food spills, sprinkle with plenty of salt while the oven is still warm (but not hot), and clear away after leaving for a while. Then wipe over with baking soda on a damp cloth.

## GREASE IS THE WORD

If you want to avoid oven cleaners containing harsh chemicals that pollute the air and waterways, but want to remove the extra grease from your oven, add vinegar to your usual natural dishwashing liquid or soap and wipe on with a clean cloth, rinsing thoroughly. Yet another green, inexpensive solution!

## Who Knew?

In ancient Egypt, baking soda was used to keep mummies smelling better and to stay fresher longer.

# A CLEAN OVEN, INSIDE AND OUT

Next time you're cleaning your oven, don't forget to also clean the oven knobs and burner rings as well. There's no need to use any sort of toxic cleanser: Simply soak the knobs and rings in a mixture of 2 cups of baking soda, 1 cup of vinegar, and 5 drops of an essential oil (try orange oil), and the grease will loosen. Then, just brush with an old toothbrush and they're clean.

# STAINED MI-CROWAVE

For stubborn stains and odors in the microwave, place a bowl of hot water with sliced lemon in the microwave. Turn on a high setting for about 5 minutes. Stand for a few minutes and then remove. Wipe inside with a soft cloth.

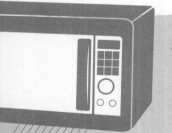

## MICROWAVE OVEN

To clean out your microwave oven, mix ½ a cup of baking soda, 1 tablespoon of white vinegar, and 4 drops of lemon oil. Apply the paste to the inside then wipe clean with a damp cloth.

## CLEANING STAINLESS STEEL

You can remove all sorts of stains and marks from stainless steel ovens with baking soda on a damp cloth. Wipe over with vinegar on a damp cloth to remove any powdery residue. Alternatively, mix a paste of baking soda and white vinegar together for tougher stains. Rub a thin layer of the paste onto the metal surface, leave for a few minutes, then rinse well and dry.

## Who Knew?

The first microwave oven was sold commercially in 1947. It cost $5000.

## INSTANT OVEN SPRAY

This is a simple, effective way to clean your oven without chemicals.

> 1 tablespoon natural dishwashing soap
>
> ½ cup distilled white vinegar
>
> warm water

Mix the natural dishwashing soap and distilled white vinegar, then add ½ cup of warm water in a spray bottle and shake well. Spray liberally on the interior of the oven. Clean the oven using a stainless steel soap pad and then rinse with clean water.

## OVERNIGHT OVEN CLEANER

Spray your oven with warm water then sprinkle a layer of baking soda on to the floor of the oven. Spray with warm water again and leave overnight. The next day, scrub the oven with a steel-wool soap pad and rinse with clean water.

## STEAM CLEAN YOUR OVEN

One simple way to clean the oven is to place an ovenproof bowl of water inside. Heat on a high temperature for 20 minutes to loosen dirt and grease. Cool slightly, and carefully wipe away condensation with a cloth. Afterwards use a cloth to smear a thin paste of baking soda and water on enamel linings. This dries to a protective layer that absorbs greasy soiling, making it easier to clean next time.

# STOVE TOP SPILLS

Wipe away spills and spattered food while still fresh. Clean up the stove top with baking soda on a damp cloth, followed by a wipe of vinegar. A drop of essential oil on any baked-on bits will easily remove them, and leave a lingering fragrance.

# CAKE PANS

To remove those dark stains that sometimes appear on cake pans, rub with a wet cloth dipped in a little borax. Then rinse the pans thoroughly before drying.

## STEAM CLEAN YOUR OVEN

One simple way to clean the oven is to place an ovenproof bowl of water inside. Heat on a high temperature for 20 minutes to loosen dirt and grease. Cool slightly, and carefully wipe away condensation with a cloth. Afterwards use a cloth to smear a thin paste of baking soda and water on enamel linings. This dries to a protective layer that absorbs greasy soiling, making it easier to clean next time.

## ALUMINUM PANS

Aluminum saucepans will come clean of stains if you drop in a few leftover lemon slices, add water, and bring to the boil and simmer for 20 minutes before washing out as normal. This will also fill your kitchen with wonderful scent neutralizing any odors.

## BURNT SAUCEPANS

For burnt food stuck to the bottom of your pan, add either a paste of baking soda and water or a paste of baking soda and lemon juice. Leave to soak, preferably overnight, and rinse clean. Alternatively add ¼ of a cup of white vinegar and 1 tablespoon of baking soda to the pan. Bring to the boil and then leave to cool. Drain off the residue and then rinse clean.

## TREATING YOU NEW CAST-IRON PANS

Before using a new cast-iron pan for the first time, wash it in soapy water, rinse, and dry thoroughly. Brush with cooking oil and heat slowly until hot but not smoking. Cool and wipe out before use. After you use you pan, always cool it completely before washing.

## WOKS NEED TLC

A well-seasoned wok needs just a light clean and lasts for years if you follow this simple procedure: Once washed, heat the wok on a burner until a few drops of water sprinkled on the surface start to move and the wok becomes darker. Once black, dip paper towel wads in sesame oil. Hold with a pair of tongs and wipe over the surface then remove. Reduce the heat to low and leave the wok to sit for 15 minutes. Turn off the heat and cool.

## NON-STICK PANS

To remove stains from non-stick pans, boil a mixture of 1 tablespoon of baking soda and 1 cup of water. Discard the liquid, and rinse the pan well. For those burnt bits that won't come away from the bottom of the pan, liberally spread a thick paste of baking soda and water and leave the pan overnight. Discard all that comes away, and wash the pan in hot water.

# REMOVE WATER MARKS

To remove hard-water marks on pots, add some water to the pot, add 1 tablespoon of cream of tartar, and simmer for 10 minutes. Rinse and wipe clean.

# STINKY KITCHEN CURE

When nasty smells threaten to overwhelm your kitchen, just boil 3 fl oz. of vinegar in a pint or two of water. The rising heat carries vinegar particles to surfaces on which cooking grease and smoke have landed and neutralizes their effect. This works particularly well when you're cooking fish.

## DIRTY POTS AND PANS, AND THE RHUBARB SOLUTION

Degreasers designed to clean your kitchen pans are often full of harsh and toxic ingredients, and should be avoided. Luckily, you can clean the bottom of your pan without resorting to toxic chemicals by covering the bottom of the pot with water, adding two stalks of chopped rhubarb, and boiling it for half an hour. The rhubarb will pull the dirt off the sides. Note: rhubarb doesn't clean aluminum pots. Try cleaning those with vinegar instead.

## PERFECTLY PRESERVED

Never use metal polish on anything to be used for cooking. Instead clean the inside of brass preserving pans with a paste made from distilled white vinegar and kitchen salt. Wash, rinse thoroughly, and dry well before using.

## NASTY LUNCH BOX GOT YOU DOWN?

Freshen up you kid's lunchbox by moistening a slice of bread with white vinegar and letting it sit in the closed lunchbox over night. In the morning, the smells should be gone.

## TRASH CAN CLEANER

To clean and disinfect your trashcan, wipe over with this solution then with a clean damp cloth. Mix 1 tablespoon of borax, 3 tablespoons of hot water, and 4 drops tea tree essential oil.

## GARBAGE CAN

Another way to keep your garbage can smelling fresh, and easier to clean when needed, is to mix ¼ of a cup of baking soda with a few drops of your favorite essential oil. Sprinkle the mixture on the bottom of a dry garbage can. It will smell fresh and will help with the job the next time you clean it out.

## CITRUS TRASH CANS ARE A GOOD THING

Wash and deodorize trashcans with a solution of 1 teaspoon of lemon juice to 1½ pints of water.

# TRASH CAN ODORS

Instead of using room fresheners or anti-smell powders and sprays in your trashcan to cut down on nasty odors, simply sprinkle a handful of salt inside. The salt acts by neutralizing unwanted smells.

## Who Knew?

In the United States, the average person produces over 4 pounds of trash per day, and up to *56 tons* of trash per year.

# STONE COUNTERTOPS

Countertops made of stone are sometimes sealed with a penetrating commercial sealant. Make sure that any surface on which you prepare food is sealed with a non-toxic sealant. Vegetable oil is an inexpensive option that is perfect for food preparation areas.

## GREASE LIGHTNING

There's no need to clean disgusting kitchen grease with expensive, toxic detergents. Simply mix equal portions of salt and baking soda on a damp towel and go to work. When mixed together, baking soda and vinegar have powerful degreasing properties, without causing any harm to the environment.

## KITCHEN SURFACE STAINS

For hard-to-beat, stubborn stains on your kitchen surfaces, dampen a sponge and apply baking soda, then wipe clean as normal. The abrasive powder will get rid of most stains, but if the mark remains, try softening the stain with a paste of baking soda and a little water before cleaning.

## FOR REALLY GREASY SURFACES

This spray is a heavy-duty version to be used to remove greasy film from kitchen walls, cabinet faces, and cupboards.

    ¼ cup of baking soda

    ½ cup distilled white vinegar

    1 teaspoon natural dishwashing soap

    water

    5 drops essential lemon oil

Mix all ingredients together in a gallon of warm water. Clean with a cloth or abrasive sponge.

## YOUR EVERYDAY SURFACE-CLEANING SPRAY

You'll use this terrific cleaner every day for walls, woodwork, and countertops.

> 1 teaspoon borax
>
> 2 tablespoons distilled white vinegar
>
> ½ teaspoon natural dishwashing soap
>
> lavender oil
>
> rosemary oil
>
> warm water

Mix the borax with 2 cups of warm water in a spray bottle and shake. Then add the distilled white vinegar, natural dishwashing soap, and 10 drops of lavender oil and 5 drops of rosemary oil. Shake the bottle again. Spray on surfaces and wipe off with a clean cloth.

## HEAT MARKS ON WOOD

Hot pots and pans can leave white marks on wooden kitchen surfaces. Rub the mark with a candle of a light or dark color depending on the color of your wood. Cover with a double layer of paper towel and press the towels with a warm iron then buff with a cloth.

# TILE REFRESHER

To clean away stains on ceramic tiles, rub with a cloth dipped in distilled white vinegar. Then wipe over with a clean, damp cloth. Alternatively, try using a cut lemon dipped in salt to rub on the tiles. This will clean tiles, remove stains, and leave your kitchen smelling fresh.

# CLEAN SHELVES

Dust the outside of your kitchen cabinets with a clean cloth and wipe with a clean, damp cloth. Remove marks on shelves by sprinkling with baking soda and wiping over with a damp cloth.

## ANOTHER GREAT SPRAY FOR A CLEAN KITCHEN

½ cup distilled white vinegar

¼ cup natural dishwashing soap

lavender essential oil

lemon essential oil

warm water

Mix the distilled white vinegar and natural dishwashing soap in to ½ cup of warm water. Add a few drops of both lavender and lemon oils in a spray bottle and shake well.

## THE KITCHEN FLOOR DEGREASER

Try this recipe for your tile floors.

½ cup distilled white vinegar

¼ cup baking soda

2 tablespoons natural dishwashing soap

eucalyptus essential oil

orange or lemon essential oil

hot water

Mix the baking soda, natural dishwashing soap and distilled white vinegar with 2 gallons of water in a bucket. Stir in 10 drops of eucalyptus oil and 5 drops of orange or lemon oil. Mix well in a bucket and wash the floor with a sponge or mop. Rinse with clean water.

## BUTCHER BLOCK COUNTERTOPS

Brighten a butcher's block with a paste made from salt and a few drops of lemon juice. With a clean cloth, rub hard enough into the wood to free food particles. Rinse and wipe clean for a fresh-smelling, inexpensive alternative to chemical cleaners.

## HOW DO YOU PROTECT YOUR WOODEN CUTTING BOARDS?

Protect wooden chopping boards from splitting by rubbing with a little vegetable oil. To remove stains, scrub well with a stiff brush and hot water. Eliminate food odors by rubbing with salt and a cut lemon. Allow boards to air dry before using again.

# FOR CLEANING YOUR WOODEN CUTTING BOARDS

Instead of using chemical cleaners, mix a paste of baking soda, lemon and warm water and apply this to your board after use, especially if chopping pungent foods. Leave for 15 minutes and then wash off.

## Who Knew?

Americans purchased almost 4 pounds of lemons per person in 2011. I wonder how many were used to clean cutting boards?

# THIS CRAZY TIP REALLY WORKS

Remove strong food smells from your hands by rubbing them under cold running water while holding a stainless steel spoon in the same way as you would soap. Rinse with soap and water. You can also simply fill an aluminum bowl with cold water, and rub your hands against the sides. It really works!

## DO YOUR HANDS STINK?

If your hands smell of fish or onions after preparing a meal, don't immediately reach for the dishwashing liquid. Salt dissolved in warm water will work just as well as any dishwashing liquid and will keep your run-off water detergent free. Another tip to remove fish smell from your hands is to wash them with a little bit of water and dry mustard.

## WHEN VEGGIES STAIN YOUR HANDS

To clean away stains left on your skin by fruit and vegetables the natural way, rub a cut lemon onto your hands, adding a little sugar for a slight abrasive action.

## LET THEM BREATHE

When storing cast iron skillets, make sure to apply a thin layer of shortening to the inside surface beforehand. Cover the interior of each skillet with a paper towel and stack, but be sure not to store your cookware with lids on. They need air in order to stay free of moisture and rust.

## THE EASIEST WAY TO CLEAN YOUR FREEZER

This formula couldn't be simpler.

> ¼ cup baking soda
>
> rosemary essential oil
>
> water
>
> white distilled vinegar

Turn up the freezer temperature (making it warmer), for 10 minutes, and leave the door open for the same amount of time. While the freezer is warming, remove any food, and pack it in ice in the sink or in a cooler. Mix together the baking soda, 1 cup of water, and 6 drops of rosemary essential oil. Use the mixture to wipe down the inside of the freezer. Then wipe over with a cloth dipped in vinegar. Finally, wipe with a dry cloth. Turn the temperature down again (to make cooler), and replace food.

## FOR THE FRESHEST FRUIT EVER

Keep your fruit and vegetables fresh by adding a couple of natural cellulose sponges to your vegetable drawer. These absorb the excess moisture and condensation, keeping the air dry. Also, keep your fruit, veggies, and herbs fresher longer by storing them in sealed, plastic bags containing a damp paper towel. It works like a charm.

# ICE BREAKER

To defrost a freezer, unplug and place bowls of hot—but not boiling— water inside. Use a wooden spoon to scrape ice away. Remove stains by using baking soda on a damp cloth. Wipe clean and dry.

# FRESHEN UP FRIDGES

Place a small cup of baking soda on one of the shelves of your fridge to remove bad smells. Remember to re-place it monthly. You can also wipe down the inside with a solution of 1 part baking soda to 7 parts water, or use a damp cloth sprinkled with a few drops of vanilla essence. All are great ways to keep your refrigerator odor-free.

## THREE STEPS TO CLEAN THE OUTSIDE OF YOUR REFRIGERATOR...

To clean the enamel exterior of your refrigerator, simply wipe down with a cloth dipped in white vinegar. Then, with a cloth dipped in baking soda, rub away the brownish marks that can form on refrigerators. Finally, wipe down with *another* clean cloth soaked white vinegar.

## ....AND A SIMPLE WAY TO CLEAN THE INSIDE, TOO

Wipe out the inside of your fridge with a mix of 2 cups of hot water, 1 tablespoon of baking soda, and ½ a cup of freshly squeezed lemon juice. Afterward, just clean with water and you're done.

## BECAUSE NONE OF US WHY MOLD IN OUR FRIDGE

To prevent mold forming on door seals, which could prevent the door from shutting fully, wipe over from time to time with distilled white vinegar on a damp cloth. To check if your refrigerator's seals are functioning properly, close a dollar bill in the door. If you can pull it out easily, consider replacing the seals. You're wasting energy if your fridge has inefficient seals.

## BONE CUTLERY HANDLES

Sometimes bone cutlery handles will stain with age. To combat those stains, rub gently with a lemon dipped in salt, then rinse the cutlery and dry thoroughly.

## KITCHEN KNIVES

To remove stains from cooks' knives, sprinkle salt on half a lemon and carefully rub along the blade. It's also a great way to remove any onion or garlic smells from the knife, too.

# CUTLERY

Avoid immersing any cutlery with handles of wood, bone, or porcelain in water. To remove stains from cutlery, rub with a damp cloth dipped in baking soda.

## Who Knew?

A simple and effective way to sharpen scissors is to fold a square of aluminum fold, and cut it 20-30 times. Unfortunately, we know of no simple ways to sharpen you knives, folks.

# THERE'S NO BETTER WAY TO START THE MORNING THAN WITH A NICE POT OF VINEGAR

Clean up the inside of your coffee pot by boiling up an equal mix of water and white vinegar. Let the mixture simmer for about 10 minutes before rinsing well.

## TEAPOT

The inside of a teapot will come clean if you rub it with damp salt and then rinse with hot water. You could also try adding 1 tablespoon of baking soda to hot water in the teapot, and leave for an hour to do its work. Then empty out some of the liquid and use a brush to scrub the surface clean. Rinse well.

## HOW DO YOU CLEAN YOUR ELECTRIC KETTLE?

If the answer is "not very well," consider this simple formula for when the element of your kettle is covered in sediment. Combine 1½ cups of distilled white vinegar, 1½ cups of water, and 3 tablespoons of salt. Boil the kettle as normal, leaving the mixture in overnight. The next day, rinse thoroughly.

## Who Knew?

It is believed that vinegar was first made by the Babylonians in 5000 BC. It was made of fermented date palms, and used in cooking.

## COFFEEMAKER

Sediment in coffeemakers can often build up, clogging the machine. Try pouring 1 cup of distilled white vinegar into the coffeemaker as if you were making coffee. Follow this with 2 full pots of water to make sure the vinegar is totally flushed out.

## FOR THE CLEANEST FRENCH PRESS

To clean, remove the plunger and unscrew the rod from the filter. Wash the filter and glass container in hot soapy water. The filter should have a neutral smell or it will affect the flavor, and baking soda will get rid of any lingering odors. Buff brass or chrome trim with a soft cloth. And don't forget how to put it back together!

# STAINED MUGS

Mugs and cups left with tea or coffee inside for too long can become stained, so scrub them with a little baking soda and a damp cloth or brush. White, non-gel toothpaste will also work.

## Who Knew?

If you buy a cup of coffee each day at drive through windows on your way to work, you'll spend on average 45 hours a year waiting in line.

# SURFACE SCRATCHES

Remove scratches on glass by rubbing a little white, non-gel toothpaste onto the surface. Finish by polishing with a soft cloth.

## HOW TO REMOVE WAX FROM GLASS

If your water glass gets hard-to-remove wax on it, place the glass in the freezer for 1 hour. The wax should chip off easily. Alternatively, heat with a hair dryer then wipe with a clean cloth. Wash as normal in hot soapy water.

## STOPPER UNBLOCKER

If the stopper is stuck in your decanter or any other glass bottle, try removing it without chemical lubricants. Put on rubber gloves to protect your hands and enhance your grip. Wrap a hot, damp cloth around the neck of the decanter to expand the glass, then slowly dribble vegetable oil round the stopper. Gently wiggle and twist the stopper to work it free.

## CRYSTAL GLASSWARE

The simplest, most natural way to wash you crystal is in a solution of ½ a cup of white vinegar and 1½ cups of hot water. Allow crystal glasses to dry naturally. Rinse in warm water with lemon juice added for extra shine and dry with a linen tea towel.

## CLOUDY CRYSTAL CRISIS?

Fear not, help is on the way. To brighten cloudy crystal, submerge a glass in a bowl of warm vinegar for 10 minutes. Rinse, dry, and hold up to the light. If it *doesn't* look cleaner, it means a chemical reaction has taken place causing the glass to become "etched," and the cloudiness cannot be fixed. If it *does* looks better, submerge all the glasses in warm white vinegar for 1 to 2 hours. Wipe with a soft, lint-free cloth. Treat any remaining cloudiness with fine-grade steel wool dipped in vinegar.

## THE DECANTER CLEANER

Fill the base of your glass decanter with hot but not boiling water and a squirt of natural dishwashing liquid. Sprinkle in some coarse salt and swirl it around to loosen any sediment. Rinse in hot water and pat dry with a towel. To remove moisture inside, insert a few rolled up paper towels, (making sure to leave a bit out of the bottle, so you can remove them) leave overnight, and remove in the morning.

## CRYSTAL CLEAR

Use a paste of lemon juice and baking soda to remove small stains from crystal. Treat tougher stains by placing 2 teaspoons of uncooked rice inside the crystal piece, add water, and swirl around before rinsing out.

### Who Knew?

The average 6-room home in the U.S. collects 40 pounds of dust each year.

# CRACKS IN CHINA—YOU WON'T BELIEVE HOW TO FIX THEM!

To remove hairline cracks in china, soak it overnight in a bowl of warm milk. Another method is to submerge the china in milk, and gently simmer it for an hour. No matter what method you use, afterwards gently hand-wash as normal and you'll find the tiny cracks have disappeared.

## STAINED CHINA

A paste of baking soda and water rubbed into stains will help remove them without scratching the china.

## BLACK SPECKS ON CHINA

If your fine china has little black specks on it and you're hesitant to use an abrasive cleanser, help is on the way. Simply apply a little baking soda to a damp cloth and rub the affected area to get rid of black specks on china. Alternatively, try white, non-gel toothpaste on a small brush.

## GOLD CHINA WARNING

Never clean fine china with gold leaf or other gold adornments in the dishwasher, or place in the microwave for any reason. The heat from either appliance can soften or melt the metal.

## DEEP FAT FRYER

The lids of most deep-fat fryers are detachable and some are dishwasher-proof. Clean inside each time you change the oil with a plastic scouring pad and natural dishwashing liquid, avoiding damage to the non-stick coating. Outside, wipe over with a damp cloth using the soapy solution.

## PASTA MAKER

Never immerse your pasta-making machine in water, because the metal parts will rust. Instead, use a dry pastry brush to remove any remaining pasta dough. Wipe clean with vegetable oil or a slightly damp cloth.

## STAINED PLASTIC STORAGE CONTAINERS?

Stains in plastic tubs used to store food can scrubbed with a paste made with baking soda and warm water, or can be bleached out by strong sunlight. In the summer, put your plastic containers out in the sun and leave for them for several hours. In addition, to remove red tomato-based stains, apply mustard overnight and then wash out thoroughly several times. Finally, to remove onion and garlic smells, just crumple up some black and white newspaper, put in the container, and seal it overnight. The smell will be gone in the morning.

# FOR THAT STINKY THERMOS

If regular washing won't remove those unpleasant smells in your Thermos, pour in a few tablespoons of vinegar or baking soda. Then fill it with hot water and leave for 30 minutes. Pour away the liquid and then rinse thoroughly.

# 3

# CARPET STAIN REMOVAL

Getting stains out of carpets can be tricky, but there's really no need to pay for expensive, toxic cleaners, rent a carpet cleaning machine, or bring in a professional. Before you resort to those solutions, try the natural formulas listed below. And remember, the trick to cleaning carpets is to *always treat stains as soon as possible*, before the stain has had time to set. We always keep club soda on hand and douse stains as soon as they appear, then treat them with the natural formulas listed below. We've organized them alphabetically, by stain, for ease of use. Remember, as with any cleaner, *always test your cleaner in an inconspicuous place* to make sure your carpet is colorfast.

## ALCOHOL

Since there are so many different types of alcohol, stains that occur from spilled drinks will differ in color and degree of difficulty of removal (see pg. 55 for red wine stains). For any alcohol spill, however, the most simple and effective course of action is to sprinkle, spray, or pour club soda onto the affected area. Then mop up the liquid with a towel. If the carpet is stained, stepping on the towel or paper will help the liquid to be well absorbed. Repeat the process until all signs of the alcohol are removed.

## BALLPOINT PEN

Using a cloth dipped in a mixture of equal parts of milk and vinegar, dab at the ballpoint pen mark until it disappears.

## BARBECUE SAUCE

Scrape away any excess, and then spray with club soda. Press a clean towel onto the area to absorb as much liquid as possible. Repeat the process if necessary to remove all traces of the stain.

## BEET STAINS

Sprinkle club soda over the stain and blot up immediately with a clean towel, stepping on the towel, if necessary, to absorb as much of the liquid as possible. Repeat until the stain has gone.

## BERRY STAINS

Sprinkle club soda over the stain and blot up immediately with a clean towel, stepping onto it to absorb as much of the liquid as possible. Repeat the process until all traces of the stain have disappeared.

## BLOOD

Never use hot water on a bloodstain! For fresh stains, sponge the area immediately with cold water. If this is not enough to treat it, pour club soda over the stained area and blot quickly with a clean towel, stepping onto it to absorb as much liquid as possible. Repeat the process until all traces of the stain have disappeared. If the stain is dry, apply a paste of borax and water to the affected area, wait for it to dry, and then brush or vacuum away. Eucalyptus oil is also effective for treating bloodstains. Drop a little onto a wet cloth, and dab at the stain until it has been removed.

**Who Knew?**

Over 90% of all carpets purchased for home use in the United States are made of nylon.

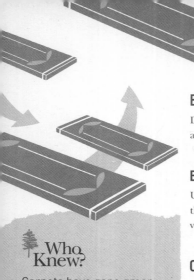

## BUBBLE GUM

Drop some eucalyptus oil on a cloth and dab at the area. Then scrape away the gum with a knife.

## BURN MARKS

Use fine steel wool or nail scissors to scrape away the burnt fibers. Then sponge the area with a little vinegar.

## CHOCOLATE

Scrape away the excess with a knife, and then spray with club soda. Press a clean towel into the area to absorb the liquid. If a stain remains, repeat the procedure until gone. Alternatively, mix equal parts of vegetable glycerin and warm water, and then gently rub this mixture into the chocolate stain. Rinse with warm water and repeat if necessary.

### Who Knew?

Carpets have gone green, too. When in the market for a new carpet, ask your dealer if they sell products certified as "Green Label" by the Carpet and Rug Institute. That means the carpet, adhesive and cushion products few VOCs (volatile organic compound).

## COFFEE

Spray club soda onto the spill and press a clean towel onto it to absorb all the liquid. Repeat the process until stain disappears.

## COSMETICS

There are many kinds of cosmetics on the market, and this simple formula works on many of them. Mix a solution of 1 tablespoon of borax dissolved in a little hot water and added to ½ a cup of water. Apply to the stain until it comes away.

## CURRY

Spray club soda on the affected area, then press a clean towel into it to absorb all liquid. Then sponge with a solution of ½ a cup of white vinegar and 1 cup of water.

# EGG

Do not use hot water on egg stains as they will cook, making them harder to remove. Instead sponge the stain with cold, salted water until the stain is removed.

## FRUIT

Sprinkle club soda over the stain and blot up immediately with a clean towel, stepping onto it to absorb as much of the liquid as possible. Repeat until all traces of the stain disappear.

## GLUE

Soak a cloth in warm water and place it over the affected area, pressing the warm water into the glue. Leave the cloth there for an hour or so, after which the glue should be soft enough to dissolve or be picked off. Repeat the process if necessary. Finish by rubbing a clean damp cloth over the area to remove any last traces. You could also try dabbing at the area with a cloth with a few drops of eucalyptus oil on it. If the glue has set and cannot be removed, use nail scissors to trim the affected area carefully away.

## GREASE

Sprinkle flour or baking soda over the stain and leave for several hours. Vacuum, and then blot with a damp cloth sprinkled with eucalyptus oil.

## HAIR DYE

As soon as a spill happens, pour or spray club soda over the area and blot with a clean cloth or towel to absorb all the liquid. Sprinkle borax over the area, leave to dry, and then vacuum.

## HONEY

Sponge up honey with warm water. If a stain remains, sprinkle with borax or baking soda. Leave to
dry, then vacuum up.

## INK

As soon as possible blot up all you can, then spray
or pour club soda over the area. Press a clean towel
onto the area to absorb as much of the liquid as possible. Sprinkle liberally with borax, leave to dry, and
then vacuum up.

## JAM AND JELLY

For jam, jelly or marmalade stains on your carpet,
wipe off the surplus then sponge with a cloth
moistened in a warm water and dishwashing liquid
solution. If the mark persists, rub on a little borax
powder, leave for a few minutes, and then sponge
clear.

## MEDICINE

For most liquid medicines, spray with club soda, and
press a clean towel onto the area to absorb as much
liquid as possible. If a stain remains, sprinkle with
borax or baking soda, leave to dry, and then vacuum.

## MILK

Mop up with a towel, and then sprinkle with baking soda. It will absorb the milk and so prevent any stale milk odor. Once the powder has dried completely, vacuum up.

## MUD

Mud stains on flooring will usually come away with a simple wipe with a wet cloth or mop. For mud stains on carpet, sprinkle liberally with baking soda. If the carpet has a long pile, gently rub the powder in with a soft brush. Leave for an hour or so, and then vacuum clean.

## MUD, TOO

Another great way to rid your carpet of mud is with shaving cream. Simply work some white, foamy shaving cream into the stain, and let it sit for 20 minutes, then blot with cold water.

## NAIL POLISH

Look out for a commercially available organic nail polish remover. To remove nail polish from the carpet, blot up as much as possible, and test the remover on an inconspicuous spot before using it to dab at the stain.

## RED WINE I

As soon as possible, pour white wine over the stained area. Then, mop up with a clean towel before dousing with club soda. Mop up again, using a fresh towel, and repeat the club soda process until all traces of the stain have disappeared.

## RED WINE II

Pour salt into the stain while it is still wet (about a half an inch layer) and let it soak the wine up. The next day, vacuum the salt up and the stain should be gone

## RUST

Sponge the rust-stained area with a mix of salt and lemon juice. Wipe with clean, damp cloth.

## SOFT DRINK

Spray with club soda, and press a clean towel into the area to absorb all the liquid. If a stain remains, dab at it with a cloth dipped in a solution of 1 tablespoon of borax and ½ a cup of water.

## Who Knew?

Want to brighten your carpet easily? Just sprinkle a bit of cornstarch on your carpet and let it sit for 1-2 hours. Vacuum afterwards, and you'll be amazed how much dirt you've removed.

## SOOT

Vacuum up as much as possible, and then sprinkle the area with salt to absorb the soot. Vacuum again. If a stain remains, sponge with warm water.

## SYRUP

Sponge with either a solution of equal quantities of vinegar and warm water or a solution of 1 cup of borax in 2 cups of hot water.

## TEA

Spray with club soda, and then mop up the liquid with a clean towel. Repeat the treatment until all traces of the stain have disappeared.

## TOMATO

Sponge with a borax solution made with 1 tablespoon of borax dissolved in a little hot water before adding 2 cups of water.

## URINE

Clean up urine on carpet or other flooring by mopping up as much liquid as possible with a clean towel. Then sprinkle liberally with baking soda, with 3 drops eucalyptus oil or tea tree oil added. Allow this to absorb what urine is left. Then vacuum, and sponge with vinegar and water to deodorize further and treat the stain.

## VOMIT

Ugh. Clean up as much as you can, and then sprinkle liberally with baking soda, and leave to dry. Vacuum the powder up, then sponge the area with white vinegar.

## WAX

If the wax is still soft, pack ice cubes around it so that it hardens. Then scrape it away with a knife. To remove any bits, place sheets of brown paper on top and use a warm iron to press the paper over the stain. Keep turning or replacing the paper as the wax comes away onto it.

### Who Knew?

Another great all purpose carpet cleaner is Ivory Soap. When all else fails, rub a little of it into the stain and scrub with an old toothbrush. It's been know to lift red wine, grape jelly, tomato sauce, and other hard-to-remove stains.

# 4

# LIVING AREAS

Most families spend a good amount of time in their living areas, watching television, reading, or simply hanging out with each other. The last thing you need to clean any area your family spends that much time in is the toxic, chemical-filled products currently on the market. Try these natural solutions instead, and rest easy.

## WONDERFUL WALL WASH

Eucalyptus oil has antifungal and antibacterial properties so this solution is great for washing down painted walls.

> 2 cups distilled white vinegar
>
> warm water
>
> eucalyptus essential oil

In a bucket mix 4 cups of warm water with the white vinegar, and 20 drops of eucalyptus (or tea tree) essential oil. Use a sponge or clean cloth to wipe down the walls, starting at the bottom and working your way to the top. Then wipe down the walls again with clean water.

## CRAYON ON THE WALLS?

That's just bad parenting, folks. Welcome to our world! The simplest way to get crayon marks off a wall is to rub gently with a damp cloth dipped in baking soda. Then wipe down with a clean cloth, and you won't have to repaint.

## MOLD ON WALLS AND CEILINGS

Wash with a solution of ¼ cup of baking soda and 1 cup of hot water, then wipe with hot vinegar. If stains are stubborn, rub with baking soda on a damp cloth.

## SPOT CLEAN WITH SODA

Matte and water-based latex painted walls may be cleaned with a paste made from 4 tablespoons baking soda and 4 tablespoons water mixed together. This removes crayon and ink marks, furniture scuffs, and grease spots. Apply, leave for 10 minutes then wipe away with a damp cloth.

## VINYL WALLPAPER

You can use warmed distilled white vinegar to wipe down vinyl wallpaper. Then wipe over with a clean damp cloth.

## NON-WASHABLE WALLPAPER, BORAX, A GUM ERASER, AND BREAD

If you have non-washable wallpaper, clean away marks by rubbing in a little borax powder and then brushing away. A gum eraser will remove many sorts of marks, as will a piece of white bread squeezed into a tight ball. Just rub the wallpaper gently with whatever solution you choose. And remember to dust your wallpaper on a regular basis.

# GREASY MARKS ON WALLPAPER

To eliminate grease on wallpaper without chemical cleaning products, first cover the area with brown paper. Apply a warm iron and the paper will absorb the grease.

# SCUFF MARKS

For scuff marks on flooring, rub with a little eucalyptus oil on a clean cloth and they should disappear.

## WASHABLE WALLPAPER

Mix 1 teaspoon of liquid castile soap and 2 cups of warm water. Wipe the wallpaper in a circular motion, covering one small area at a time. Then wipe over with a damp clean cloth. Avoid saturating the paper when washing it down.

## LAMINATE

Stains can be removed from laminated surfaces by rubbing with baking soda on a damp cloth. Finish with a wipe of vinegar to clean away any powdery deposits and leave the laminate shining clean.

## LINOLEUM

To clean linoleum floors, mix 3 cups of white vinegar, 12 cups of hot water, and 20 drops of pine essential oil. Sponge or mop onto the linoleum being careful not to over-wet.

## SHEEPSKIN RUG

Rub a little baking soda into the stain and leave before brushing away or shaking it out. For more stubborn stains, sponge with a solution of 1 tablespoon of borax in 1 cup of warm water. Then sponge with a cloth dipped in vinegar, and dry the rug outdoors.

## VINYL FLOORING

It's easy to clean all your vinyl floors with this simple formula.

>   ¾ cup liquid castile soap (available at health food stores)
>
>   1½ cup distilled white vinegar
>
>   tea tree oil
>
>   water

Mix 12 cups of hot water with the liquid castile soap and the white vinegar. Add 20 drops of tea tree oil and mix well. Apply to floor with mop or sponge then rinse clean.

## DEODORIZE CARPETS

It is possible to fully clean and deodorize carpets without resorting to chemical carpet cleaners or shampoo. Simply vacuum, liberally sprinkle cornstarch or baking soda, leave one hour, then vacuum again. To remove tough stains, try cold club soda or repeatedly blot with vinegar and soapy water instead of automatically reaching for the stain remover.

# A CLEAN FLOOR BREWING

You can clean wooden floors and bring up the shine, particularly on older wooden flooring, by using tea. Brew 2 teabags in hot water and cool to room temperature, and then apply with a mop or a cloth. The added bonus is that there's no need to rinse. Only use this on hardwood flooring to bring out the natural grain and luster.

## Who Knew?

To remove scuff marks from most kinds of flooring, just dab a little eucalyptus essential oil on a clean cloth and rub away.

## Who Knew?

The Environmental Protection Agency has ranked indoor air pollution among the top 5 environmental dangers to the public. It found that indoor air can be 2 to 5 times more polluted than the worst outside air.

# WHEN YOUR VACUUM BAG IS NOT SO FRESH

If your vacuum's filter bag smells less than fresh, next time you vacuum add a few drops of your favorite essential oil on the filter bag. It will give your home a wonderful smell while cleaning.

## WANT TO FRESHEN UP YOUR CARPETS EASILY?

Don't use a commercial vacuuming powder on your carpets as these contain talc and chemicals that add to air pollution. Instead, simply fill a spray bottle with water and a few drops of your favorite essential oil. Spray lightly on the carpet. It really does the trick.

## FOR THE CLEANEST WOODEN FLOORS

Forget the store-bought wooden floor cleaners. Just mix a batch of this formula and start saving.

½ cup distilled white vinegar

2 tablespoons natural dishwashing soap

Mix the distilled white vinegar and natural dishwashing soap into a bucket with 2 gallons of warm water. Add in 10 drops of lavender oil and 5 drops of orange oil, and stir. Mop your wooden floor with the liquid then mop with clean water afterwards. Take care not to over-wet.

## SIMPLE CARPET SHAMPOO

It might be simple, but it really works.

> ½ cup dishwashing liquid
>
> 2 pints distilled white vinegar
>
> water

Mix the dishwashing liquid into 2 cups of boiling water. Cool and a jelly will form. Use a damp sponge to rub this gently into the area that needs cleaning. Rinse with a solution of 2 cups of distilled white vinegar and a quart of water applied with a clean cloth. Wipe dry with another cloth and repeat as necessary.

## SLATE

Wipe slate with a few drops of lemon oil to make it shine. Polish with a soft dry cloth. To remove oil stains, sprinkle with a liberal amount of flour and leave for 10 minutes. Scrub with warm water and natural dishwashing liquid soap. Oil slate worktops once or twice a year with linseed oil and buff until dry.

## THE ON-THE-GO WOODEN FLOOR CLEANER

If your floor is not especially dirty, try this no-rinse-required version instead. Mix 2 gallons of warn water with ¼ of a cup of distilled white vinegar and 15 drops of lavender oil in a bucket and mop floor as required.

# RUBBER SOLE MARKS

If your shoes have left black marks all over the floor, try rubbing out the marks with a pencil eraser. For vinyl floors, smear baby oil over the mark: Wait a few minutes and wipe the marks clean away, making sure all excess oil is removed from the floor to avoid it being slippery.

# UNSEALED FLOORBOARDS

To polish floorboards that have been stained but not varnished or painted, apply a little linseed or olive oil directly on the wood and dry with a clean cloth. This can also be used on wooden furniture.

## VARNISHED FLOOR CLEANER

This is also works great on lacquered surfaces.

2 tablespoons olive oil

1 tablespoon distilled white vinegar

Mix the oil and vinegar in a spray bottle, and add a quart of warm (not hot) water. Spritz floors and furniture lightly and dry with a damp cloth.

## STONE FLOORS

Never use soap on stone floors. It cannot be absorbed, so soap can make the floor really slippery. Instead, clean with a solution of 1 pint of water to 1 tablespoon of washing soda, then mop with clean water.

## TERRACOTTA WARNING

Soap can make unglazed and terracotta tiles cloudy, so never clean these tiles with soap. Instead, try equal portions of water and distilled white vinegar. Terracotta can also be treated with baking soda and a damp sponge. Remove hard-water spots with a soft cloth. Finish by polishing with a soft, dry cloth.

## FOAMING FABRIC CLEANER

This gentle foaming cleaner is great for spot cleaning fabric.

¼ cup natural dishwashing liquid

Lavender essential oil

Warm water

Mix together the natural dishwashing liquid and warm water, and add 6 drops of lavender oil in a bowl. Using a whisk or mixer, beat into stiff foam. Apply the foam to soiled areas then remove with a damp cloth. Vacuum if needed.

## ALCOHOL SPILLS ON FURNITURE

Act quickly to soak up the spilled liquid with an old towel. Then, in the case of wooden furniture, a little olive oil rubbed into the grain will revive it. For other furniture, add a few drops of your favorite essential oil to a damp cloth, and wipe down.

## HOW ANNOYING ARE STICKY, ADHESIVE LABELS?

We say really, really annoying. However, sticky labels will come away easily if you apply a little eucalyptus or tea tree oil, and rub gently with a cloth. You could also try peanut butter or vegetable oil —both will loosen some labels very effectively. To get sticky labels off of wood surfaces, apply vegetable oil liberally to the label, leave overnight, and then rub with a soft cloth. The labels should come right off.

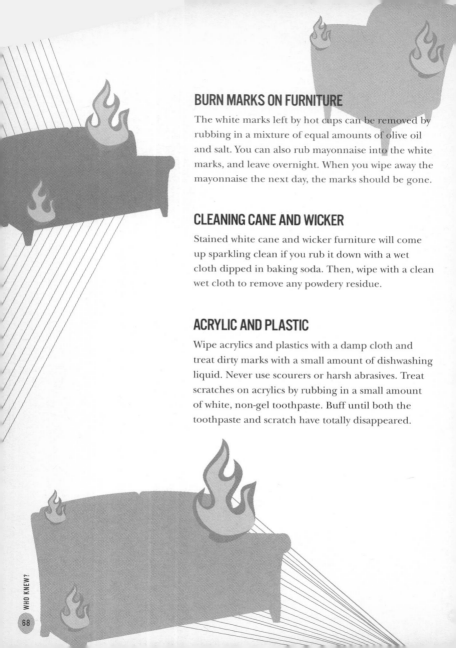

## BURN MARKS ON FURNITURE

The white marks left by hot cups can be removed by rubbing in a mixture of equal amounts of olive oil and salt. You can also rub mayonnaise into the white marks, and leave overnight. When you wipe away the mayonnaise the next day, the marks should be gone.

## CLEANING CANE AND WICKER

Stained white cane and wicker furniture will come up sparkling clean if you rub it down with a wet cloth dipped in baking soda. Then, wipe with a clean wet cloth to remove any powdery residue.

## ACRYLIC AND PLASTIC

Wipe acrylics and plastics with a damp cloth and treat dirty marks with a small amount of dishwashing liquid. Never use scourers or harsh abrasives. Treat scratches on acrylics by rubbing in a small amount of white, non-gel toothpaste. Buff until both the toothpaste and scratch have totally disappeared.

## VINYL

Vinyl upholstery will clean up well if you simply wash it with warm soapy water. For a little extra power, try a mix of 1 tablespoon of liquid castile soap, 2 tablespoons of white vinegar, and 1 cup of warm water. Apply with a damp cloth, and then finish by wiping with clean, soft cloth.

## MAKE YOUR OWN POLISH

Most mass-produced furniture polishes contain solvents that are harmful to the environment. Many of them come in aerosol sprays, which are wasteful and contain harmful gases. Make your own polish by melting 2 tablespoons of paraffin wax with 2 pints of mineral oil and a few drops of lemon oil, then apply as normal and polish the surface when dry.

# HOW DO YOU GET RID OF WATER RINGS ON WOODEN FURNITURE?

Instead of using chemical treatments for wood, or varnishes that contain air-polluting chemicals, get rid of rings on your wooden furniture by rubbing the mark with olive or almond oil, or mix butter with cigarette ash to turn it brown. For either treatment, rub the furniture with soft, dry cloth, then polish afterwards.

# WALNUT WOOD WONDER

Another way to remove white rings on your wood surfaces is to rub the mark with half a raw walnut. It really works, and you won't have to reach for chemical polish.

## WATER STAINS, MAYO AND BAKING SODA

Another great way of removing water stains on your wooden surfaces is to mix mayonnaise and baking soda into a thick paste. Rub a small amount of the paste into the wood and leave for 5 minutes. Wipe off and buff with a soft cloth.

## CANDLE WAX

When spilled candle wax has cooled on a wooden surface, carefully scrape off the excess with a blunt knife. Wash off any remaining residue with hot soapy water and allow to dry. Finish by polishing the area.

## TWO NATURAL WAYS TO REMOVE SCRATCHES

Remove smaller scratches on wooden furniture by rubbing in a mixture of strained lemon juice and vegetable oil in equal quantities. For deeper scratches, melt a few drops of a wax crayon that matches your furniture color into the scratch. Smooth the wax into the scratch and scrape away any excess. Buff the area with furniture polish.

## THE BAMBOO, WILLOW, AND RATTAN SOLUTION

It is important to regularly vacuum and dust all your bamboo, rattan, and willow furniture to keep it look it's best. To clean it, wipe with water and a natural dishwashing liquid solution, taking care not to over-wet the surface; finish by drying with a cloth. Since this type of furniture needs to retain moisture, periodically spray it with water, too.

## UPHOLSTERY

Clean and dust upholstery regularly to prevent dust from building up, and use this foam cleaner for spring cleaning.

> 1 teaspoon borax
>
> 2 tablespoons natural dishwashing soap
>
> lavender oil
>
> water

Dissolve the borax in ¼ cup of hot water. Allow to cool to room temperature, and then add the natural dishwashing soap and 3 drops of lavender oil. Beat with a whisk to create a foam. Working on a small section of your upholstery at a time, rub in the foam and immediately wipe clean with a damp cloth, then it leave to dry.

# LEATHER

To clean and condition your leather furniture, try mixing 2 tablespoons of distilled white vinegar, 2 tablespoons of extra virgin olive oil, and 2 drops of lemon oil, and shake well. After testing on an inconspicuous area, rub sparingly into your leather and buff off with a soft cloth.

# EGGS AND LEATHER, ANYONE?

Another great way to clean leather is with egg whites. Just blend the egg whites gently together, and sparingly apply to your leather with a clean cloth. Buff afterwards with another clean cloth.

# PREVENT POLISH DEPOSITS

Layers of polish can build up on wooden furniture and leave a dull finish. To remove excess product build up, mix together 2 tablespoons of distilled white vinegar and 2 tablespoons of water. Apply to the surface with a soft cloth and wipe off at once.

## BEESWAX

Protect the finish of wooden furniture by applying a good-quality natural beeswax polish at least once a year, twice if your furniture is used heavily. Apply sparingly with a soft cloth, and polish afterwards with another lint-free cloth. Rub it again for a good shine, rather than adding layer upon layer of wax.

## IT'S LIKE A FACELIFT FOR YOUR CANE FURNITURE

Tighten up stretched and sagging cane by sponging carefully on the upper and lower sides with hot soapy water. Leave to dry away from heat—preferably in the open air— where it will shrink back to its original shape.

## WICKER

Use wire cutters to trim any broken wicker. To clean wicker, fill a spray bottle filled with water and 1 tablespoon of distilled white vinegar, spray, and then wipe clean, using a cotton swab or toothbrush for crevices. If possible, dry outdoors in the sun, and keep away from direct heat sources indoors. Avoid sitting in your cleaned wicker chair for two or three days after cleaning, as that can cause sagging.

## FOR ALL YOUR GLASS AND PLASTIC FURNITURE

Glass and plastic furniture creates a real sense of space in your home but needs to be cleaned regularly to look at its best. Using a spray bottle, spray a solution of 1 part white vinegar to 4 parts water onto a cloth. Rub into the glass or plastic, taking care not to hold onto the article and leave greasy finger marks.

## LACQUERED FURNITURE

Wipe lacquered furniture with a damp (but not wet) cloth. Dry with another clean cloth and buff to a shine with a soft cloth. An occasional polish with a natural, homemade solution adds shine to a dull surface.

## IT THERE ANYTHING BAKING SODA CAN'T DO?

A quick and easy way of freshening up your sofa is to sprinkle a little baking soda beneath the cushions. The baking soda absorbs any odors. Leave for at least 15 minutes, and then vacuum it away.

# NUTS ABOUT WOODEN FURNITURE

You can treat scratched surfaces on wooden furniture by rubbing them with a halved nut—try Brazilian, pecan, peanuts or walnuts, depending on the color of your furniture. You can also get rid of small dents by placing a dampened cloth on top and running over carefully with a steam iron. (I'd be careful before trying it on valuable antiques, though.)

# STICKING DRAWERS?

For an easy way to prevent drawers from sticking without reaching for a chemical lubricant spray, rub a wax candle across the runners of the affected drawer. Then see the difference this will make for yourself.

## STICKING DRAWERS II

Many times drawers get stuck because humidity in the air has caused the wood to expand. To combat this, just turn on a 60-watt bulb, encased in a plastic lamp guard, and put it bulb-side up in the drawer for an hour or two. That should do the trick.

## CORK

To remove stains from cork without damaging it, scrub a piece of dry bread over the surface. Alternatively, pat grimy spots with light masking tape. Clean by wiping with a damp cloth and warm soapy water.

## LAMINATED FURNITURE

Coat stubborn stains on laminated furniture with a paste of baking soda and water. Leave for several hours and then rub briskly before wiping off. White, non-gel toothpaste also does the same trick.

## CLEAN YOUR BOOKS WITH CORN STARCH

You can remove mildew stains from books by dabbing gently with a weak vinegar solution of 1 tablespoon of white vinegar in ½ a cup of water. In addition, it's a good idea to dust mildewed areas on books with cornstarch, and then let them air out for a day or two. Afterwards, dust the powder away before placing the books back on their shelves. To help prevent mildew from affecting books, allow enough room around them for air to circulate when storing.

## DUSTING BOOKS

Remove dust from books with a clean, soft, slightly damp paintbrush or make-up brush. Take each book individually off the shelf; dust outward from the binding. It's fine to flip the pages to dust them—just avoid banging them together.

# GREASE MARKS

Place a piece of brown paper on either side of a page of a book affected with grease spots. Press gently with a warm iron to remove the grease.

## Who Knew?

About 3.1 billion books were sold in the United States in 2011.

# BRASS CURTAIN RINGS

To clean up brass curtain rings, soak them in a solution of ½ a cup of warm white vinegar and ½ a cup of warm water for 30 minutes. Then rinse, and dry thoroughly.

## CURTAINS

Curtains tend to become more easily stained over time if they are not vacuumed regularly. For washable curtains that need a good wash, remove all accessories and soak in a tub of cold water to help soften the fabric and allow the grime to surface. Then machine wash gently using liquid castile soap. Dry outdoors, but not in direct sunlight.

## THE GELATIN SOLUTION

Need to wash your sheer curtains but dread the thought of ironing them afterwards? Just run them in the washing machine on gentle cycle, and in the final rinse, pour in a packet of unflavored, clear gelatin. That will relax the fibers in your curtains, and they'll have a lot less wrinkles.

## BRIGHTEN BANISTERS

Dust painted banisters with a soft cloth dampened with a solution of warm soapy water. Rinse section by section and wipe with a dry cloth. To restore moisture to wooden banisters, try this natural polish recipe: Mix ½ a cup of olive oil, 1 tablespoon of white vinegar, and 4 drops of rose oil and apply with a soft cloth.

## BRING YOUR UMBRELLA TO THE DINING ROOM

The best way to clean an intricate glass chandelier is to dust it with a 50-50 mix of water and white vinegar. But before spraying, hang an umbrella under the chandelier, hooking the handle over an arm of the chandelier to catch the dirty water.

## CRYSTAL CHANDELIERS

First switch off the chandelier and then lightly dampen a chamois with water. Wipe down the crystals while attached to the frame; wipe the chandelier itself with a dry cloth. If the crystal is really dirty, remove and soak in a combination of warm water, 1½ tablespoons of white vinegar, and 1 drop of dishwashing liquid. Rinse under running water and buff with a soft cloth.

# LAMPSHADES

The fabric part of lampshades will come clean of stains if you sprinkle on a little baking soda or borax, leave for a few seconds, and then use a soft brush to dust the powder away.

## Who Knew?

Bill Lear (1902–1978) was an American inventor best known for founding the Lear Jet Corporation. He also named his daughter Shanda—that's right, Shanda Lear.

## CLEANING FIREPLACE BRICKS

We all know that the bricks around a fireplace can become stained over time. To combat this, wash the bricks with hot white vinegar before wiping down with a clean wet cloth. Of course, only do this when you're not using the fireplace.

## CINNAMON AND CEDARWOOD ROASTING ON AN OPEN FIRE

Try adding a few drops of your favorite essential oil directly onto logs before burning them in the fire-place. Cinnamon and cedarwood are good choices. You can also add fresh herbs to the fire to release a wonderful smell.

## CLEAN BRICKS WITH COLA

This is the best way we know to brighten up the soot-stained bricks around your fireplace.

> 12 oz. can of cola
>
> 3 fl oz. homemade all-purpose cleaner
>
> water

Mix the cola in a bucket with the homemade all-purpose household cleaner and 2 gallons of hot water. Sponge the solution onto the sooty brick and leave for 15 minutes. Loosen the soot by scrubbing with a stiff-bristled brush, and then sponge with clean water. For a stronger solution, just add more cola.

## CITRUS AND LAVENDER AIR FRESHENER

There's no need to buy the chemical-laden air fresheners available in the supermarket. Try this natural formula instead.

    1 teaspoon vodka

    lavender oil

    grapefruit oil

    water

Mix the vodka with 10 drops of both lavender and grapefruit oils in a spray bottle. Shake well, add 2 cups of water, and then and shake again. Spray the mist in the air, avoiding spraying directly on fabrics or wood.

## ANTISEPTIC AIR FRESHENER

Here's a stronger, antiseptic air freshener for really tough smells.

    eucalyptus oil

    lavender oil

    juniper oil

    water

    1 teaspoon vodka

Mix the vodka with 20 drops each of eucalyptus, lavender, and juniper oils in a spray bottle. Shake well, add 2 cups of water, and then shake again. Spray the mist in the air, avoiding spraying directly on fabrics.

# FRAGRANT HUMIDITY

We all know that to humidify your room, all you need to do is place a bowl of water on top of a radiator. Not only does it add moisture, it makes the room warmer, saving you heat. Next time, try and add a few drops of your favorite oil, and you'll have a lovely fragrance in the air while counteracting the drying nature of the heat in your home.

# A VANILLA ROOM FRESH-ENER AND THE " I'VE BEEN BAKING SCAM" ALL TOGETHER

For a wonderful, homey smell, just place a few drops of vanilla extract on a cloth or cotton ball in a small saucer. Refresh the scent when the fragrance starts to fade. To create a smell that says, "I've been baking all afternoon," dab a few drops of vanilla on a cool light bulb in your living room, and turn on the light.

## A FRUITY IDEA FOR A SMOKY ROOM

Placing a sliced apple in an enclosed area will remove the smell of cigarette smoke. Try placing a bowl of apple slices on a table or mantelpiece. Remove the apple when the smoke smells have gone. Baking soda sprinkled in an ashtray also absorbs cigarette smells in no time. Don't be tempted to just mask the smell with a chemical air-freshener when you can absorb it naturally!

## HOUSE PLANT SPRAY

A good spray for houseplants can be made using comfrey tea, which is available in health food stores and on the internet. Put 2 tablespoons of dried comfrey leaves in a bowl and pour over 2 cups of boiling water. Leave to cool, strain, and pour into a spray bottle, and spray plants once a week making sure to avoid any contact with any fabrics to avoid staining.

## GOT APHIDS?

A great way to clean houseplants is to rub the leaves with milk. (It also kills aphids.) You can also clean the leaves with a cup of baking soda in a gallon of water.

## PASTA PARTY

Your houseplants need nourishment, particularly in the dead of winter when the sunlight is limited, yet there's no need to buy expensive plant food. Just remember to save the water when you boil potatoes or pasta, let it cool, and use it to water your plants. They love the starchy water.

## FLOWER POWER

To prolong the life of cut flowers without using commercial plant food, add 2 tablespoons of vinegar and 1 teaspoon of sugar to the water. An aspirin or two in the water is also said to work. With either formula, it's a good idea to add a few pennies to the water as well. And don't forget to change the water every few days.

## ARTIFICIAL FLOWERS

To revitalize artificial flowers before reaching for cleaning products, pour salt into a large paper bag, place the flowers inside with their heads down, and shake vigorously. The dirt will be transferred to the salt. Revive paper flowers by applying a steam iron on the lowest setting.

# VASE BRIGHTENERS

Remove stubborn stains from the base of a glass vase by swirling a mixture of vinegar, with sea salt or uncooked rice, inside. The salt or rice will gently scour the surface of the glass while the vinegar breaks down deposits. This can also be used on glass cruets.

# 5

# BATHROOM

There are literally hundreds of chemical-filled products on the marker to clean your bathroom. *You don't need any of them.* Check out the natural alternatives below.

# A SIMPLE TOILET CLEANER

Pour 1 cup of borax and ¼ of a cup of lemon juice into the bowl overnight. The next day, scrub with a toilet brush and then flush. If the bowl is stained, try making a paste of borax and lemon juice and rubbing on the inside of the bowl. Leave overnight and then scrub and rinse.

## ANTI-GERM TOILET CLEANER

Try this effective natural cleaner around the toilet area, where germs love to breed.

> ¼ cup liquid castile soap
>
> 1 teaspoon eucalyptus or tea tree essential oil
>
> water

In a spray bottle, mix 2 cups of water with the liquid castile soap, and essential oil. Spray on and wipe with a clean cloth.

## LIMESCALE

Avoid cleaning your toilet with limescale remover as it contains harsh chemicals that harm the environment when flushed down the toilet into the water system. White vinegar is an excellent substitute; scrub off limescale marks with a brush dipped in vinegar.

## STUBBORN MINERAL DEPOSITS

If you have stubborn mineral deposits in your toilet bowl that will not come off with lemon juice and borax, try buffing them off with pumice stone or fine steel wool. Scoop out any water to get to the stains, dampen the porcelain, and gently scrub off the stains.

## SAVE WATER

To save water by not flushing the toilet every time, you can instead use scented vinegar. Pour 1 cup of distilled white vinegar with a couple of drops of your favorite essential oil added, down the toilet as this will break down the urine and smell fresh.

## BOWL CLEANER

Sprinkle borax or baking soda in the bowl to clean your toilet. Dampen with a little water to make a paste. Scrub with a toilet brush. Alternatively, make a paste from lemon juice and borax. Leave for 2 hours then scrub thoroughly.

# CLEAN WITH COLA

Toilet bowls can be cleaned with old, flat cola. Pour a can into the bowl, leaving it in for at least an hour before flushing. Limescale will dissolve easily and your bowl will shine.

# PREVENT STAINING

To prevent nasty black streaks appearing in the toilet and make cleaning easier, pour ½ a cup of vinegar into the bowl and leave overnight.

## DRIPPING FAUCET?

To remove the marks left by a dripping faucet, apply a paste of borax and water. Leave for 1 hour before rinsing. Repeat if necessary, leaving the paste on for a longer time the second time around.

# RUST STAINS

Make a paste of cream of tartar and lemon juice and rub into any rust stains on porcelain sinks or baths. Rinse well.

## GET JUICY WITH LIMESCALE

Don't buy any of the popular limescale removers available at your supermarket. All of them are filled with chemicals. Instead, clean the limescale off your bathroom faucets by using a clean, soft cloth soaked in lemon juice or use half a cut lemon. The lime scale will disappear in no time at all and what's more, the room will smell great.

## Who Knew?

According to a recent survey of over 1000 American mothers, the bathroom is a haven for multi-tasking for most moms. While in the bathroom, moms are reading (72.6%), talking on the phone (66%), meditating (26.2%), watching TV (25.6%), drinking coffee or eating (17.9%), and balancing the check book (6.2%). And some actually write letters (3.6%)!

## LIQUID SOAP

Plastic liquid soap dispensers are a great choice when it comes to hygiene, but bad in terms of packaging. Make your own liquid soap by putting a bar of soap in boiling water. Decant the resulting liquid in order to reuse your plastic dispensers.

## MAKE YOUR OWN HAND SOAP

Oils such as lavender, lemon, and eucalyptus are naturally antiseptic. Try adding 30 drops of lavender, 20 drops of eucalyptus, and 10 drops of lemon to a bottle of natural liquid hand soap. Don't forget to mix it well before using.

## SAY 'AHHH'

When it comes to cleaning your tile floor, grab the mouthwash. Yep, the mouthwash. Just mix about 1 cup of mouthwash in with about a gallon of warm water and mop away. Not only will the mouthwash clean the floor, but it will fight the bacteria that builds up there, too.

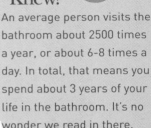

### Who Knew?

An average person visits the bathroom about 2500 times a year, or about 6-8 times a day. In total, that means you spend about 3 years of your life in the bathroom. It's no wonder we read in there.

# STAINLESS STEEL FAUCET

Stainless steel faucets or sinks can be quickly and easily cleaned with vodka. Dab a little on a sponge or cloth and wipe. Your stainless steel will come up sparkling clean.

## CHROME

Water spots can be removed from chrome bathroom fittings by mixing equal parts of baking soda and distilled white vinegar and applying to the chrome. Let it dry then polish with a soft cloth. Flour also cleans chrome well.

## PORCELAIN

Steel wool and scouring powders will scratch porcelain, so instead rub a freshly cut lemon on the surface to cut through grease and then rinse with water. Alternatively, sprinkle with baking soda and rub with a damp sponge. Neutralize with a rinse of vinegar or lemon juice, and then rinse with water.

## THE LUSH'S WAY TO CLEAN GLASS SHOWER DOORS

A great way to clean your glass shower doors is simply to wash it in leftover white wine, and then finish by buffing with a clean, dry cloth.

## THREE WAYS TO CLEAN YOUR SHOWER CURTAIN

To remove both mildew stains and soap build-up, scrub nylon shower curtains with warm vinegar. Then wash in warm soapy water, rinse, and hang out to dry in the fresh air. You can help prevent the growth of mildew on shower curtains by soaking them in a tub of water to which you've added 1 cup of salt. You can also launder your shower curtain in warm water, natural detergent, and a big white towel. The towel rubs against the curtain and scrubs it clean, so you don't have to.

## MORE SHOWER CURTAIN CLEANERS

Another way to clean your shower curtain effectively is to mix ½ a cup of borax, ½ a cup of distilled white vinegar, and 3 drops of eucalyptus oil. Use a soft brush to apply the mixture to the shower curtain. Rinse with clean water.

## SIT AND PONDER THIS TIP

If you live in an area with hard water consider this: When you leave home for more than a day or two, pour one cup of distilled white vinegar into your toilet, and cover the bowl with plastic wrap. It should prevent hard water marks from forming. When you return home, just remember to remove the wrap before…oh, forget it.

# GLASS SHOWER DOOR CLEANER II

To clean away soap build-up, rub glass shower doors with a mixture of salt and lemon juice, or borax and lemon juice. Rinse with clean water.

# SHOWERHEAD

If your showerhead is clogged with deposits, unscrew it and place it in a sealed plastic bag or old coffee can, and then cover it in equal parts of distilled white vinegar and warm water. Leave for one hour and then scrub with a brush if needed.

## Who Knew?

According to FEMA, you should avoid showering or bathing in a thunderstorm. Plumbing and bathroom fixtures can conduct electricity.

## THE MILDEW MAKER

The damp warmth of your bathroom is the perfect environment for growing mildew, so it's important to stop it from ever taking hold. One good tip is to always hang wet towels and washcloths after use; don't leave your wet washcloth in a ball in the tub. Wet towels and washcloths are hot spots for mildew growth, so always hang towels, clothing and anything that can collect moisture.

## SPEAKING OF SHOWERS, WANT TO BOOST YOUR CIRCULATION NEXT TIME YOU'RE SHOWERING?

To boost your circulation without using expensive, chemical-based lotions or potions, try alternating hot and cold water when in the shower. This also has been shown to be effective in strengthening your immune system and promotes detoxification. Try 2 or 3 minutes of very warm water, followed by 1 minute of cooler water.

## GIVE THEM SPACE

Never leave shower curtains bunched up after use, especially in a small bathroom, because the steam encourages mildew. If small spots of mildew appear, dab with baking soda on a damp cloth. If larger areas appear, rub the curtain with lemon juice, and dry in the sun if possible.

## WHAT'S THE NASTIEST PART OF YOUR BATHROOM?

It might be a horse race, but our vote goes to our shower door runners. To clean them effectively, scrub the runners with white toothpaste and an old toothbrush. Rinse by brushing with vinegar. You can also dip a stiff-bristled paintbrush in vinegar and scrub thoroughly.

## BATHTUB RINGS GOT YOU DOWN?

Cheer up. There's plenty of ways to get your bathtub clean without resorting to nasty chemicals. We've tried lemon, toothpaste, hair conditioner, and even mayonnaise! All are effective at getting grime and grease off of the bathtub.

# PREVENT BUILD-UP

Apply mineral oil all over shower doors and tiled surfaces. This delays mineral build-up and cuts down on cleaning time.

# HAS MOLD GOT A HOLD?

If you have mold in your bathroom, try this strong solution that uses tea tree oil. Mix 1 cup of borax with 2 cups of hot water and let it cool to room temperature. Add a few drops of tea tree oil and apply to the affected areas with a brush. Leave for a few hours then rinse off.

## BATHROOM CLEANER

Keep this all-purpose bathroom spray handy. You'll use it often.

 1 teaspoon borax
 ½ teaspoon natural dishwashing soap
 3 tablespoons distilled white vinegar
 lavender, eucalyptus and lemon oil
 water

Mix the borax in 2 cups of hot water and let it cool to room temperature. Pour into a spray bottle and add the dishwasher soap, distilled white vinegar, 15 drops of lavender oil, 10 drops of eucalyptus oil, and 5 drops of lemon oil. Shake well.

## MOLD AND MILDEW SPRAY

You can prevent mold and mildew from taking hold in your bathroom by cleaning regularly with this antibacterial spray.

 2 tablespoons borax
 ¼ cup distilled white vinegar
 lavender and eucalyptus oil
 water

Mix 1¾ cups of hot water with the borax and let it cool to room temperature. Pour into a spray bottle and add the distilled white vinegar, and a few drops each of lavender and eucalyptus oils. Shake well and use to clean your bathroom, scrubbing tiles and caulk with a brush, and the mold should disappear. To ensure that it doesn't return, keep your bathroom well ventilated.

## A GREAT BATHTUB CLEANER

For porcelain, enamel, and fiberglass bathtubs, try this simple formula.

> ⅓ cup baking soda
>
> ⅓ cup borax
>
> 1 teaspoon natural dishwashing soap
>
> lavender and eucalyptus oil

Mix the baking soda, borax, and natural dishwashing soap, with 5 drops each of lavender and eucalyptus oils. Do not dilute. Rub the paste on a clean cloth and go to work on your tub and sink.

## BLEACH THE NATURAL WAY

If you have a stained bath, try this bleaching formula. Mix ½ a cup of baking soda, ½ a teaspoon of natural dishwashing soap, and 1 teaspoon of hydrogen peroxide, which is a very mild bleach. Wet the surface of the bath and apply with a cloth. Rinse well with clean water.

## ANOTHER GREAT GROUT CLEANER

Another great way to clean your grout is with a mixture of ½ cup of baking soda, ½ cup of borax, and ⅓ of a cup of distilled white vinegar. Scrub the grout between tiles with the paste using an old toothbrush and rinse well.

# BATHTUB STAINS

White vinegar is perfect for tough, hard-to-shift stains and its disinfectant properties make it a great all-round cleaner. Remove stubborn bathtub stains with a solution of 1 part distilled white vinegar to 5 parts water.

## ENAMEL

Remove stains from enamel with borax on a cut lemon. Do not use scourers or strong bleach on enamel. For tough stains, try a paste of baking soda and hydrogen peroxide. Rub in and leave to dry, and then rinse off.

## MARBLE MAGIC

Never use detergent on marble, or the surface could be damaged. Marble simply needs washing with a natural dishwashing liquid soap and warm water. For stubborn stains, though, try this formula.

> 1 pint distilled white vinegar
>
> eucalyptus oil
>
> water

Mix the distilled white vinegar in ½ a pint of hot water, and add 20 drops of eucalyptus oil. Pour into a spray bottle, shake, and spray onto a soft, damp cloth and rub over the marble. Be sure to rinse thoroughly as a build-up can damage the stone. Always buff with a soft cloth until completely dry.

## GREEN STAIN REMOVAL

Tackle blue or green tinged stains on baths and showers (normally caused by water with a high copper content) by mixing a paste of equal amounts of cream of tartar and baking soda. Rub into the stain, leave for 30 minutes, and rinse well with water. Repeat if needed.

## STEAM AWAY SMELLS

To remove the smoky smells from clothes after a night out, add 1 cup of vinegar to a bathtub of hot water. Hang the clothes above the steam for an hour or so. It really works!

## DOES YOUR CAR SMELL OF SMOKE?

Speaking of smoke…we just have to a pass along this tip: the simplest way to rid your car of the smell of smoke is to put unused ground coffee in a sock, knot it, and leave it under the seat for a few days. The odor will go away almost immediately, but if you remove it, in a few hours it will come back. Leave it in the car for a few days, and the smell will disappear for good!

# WATERMARKS

To get rid of watermarks in your bathroom, try wiping distilled white vinegar or lemon juice on the affected area. Leave to get to work if needed, then rinse.

# BATHROOM FLOOR

One great way to clean your tile bathroom floor is to dissolve ¼ of a cup of borax in 1 gallon of hot water. Add 5 drops of patchouli oil and stir. Grab a clean mop and watch your floor sparkle.

## ANTISEPTIC SPRAY

This spray can be used for cleaning anything including floors, toys, and toilet seats. Fill a spray bottle nearly full of water (purified is best if possible) and then add three tablespoons of natural liquid soap. Add 30 drops of tea tree oil and shake.

## BLOCKED DRAIN?

If water is not draining away properly from your bath or shower, pull out any hair your find there. If you think there might be a hair and soap blockage further down, try bending a metal coat hanger with pliers to form a hook and try to pull out the hair.

## THE WASHING SODA/BAKING SODA ONE-TWO PUNCH

If the water isn't going down the drain, pour a cup of washing soda over the drain area and let it set for a while to work its way down to the clog. Once the clog is loosened, pour 1 cup of baking soda followed by 3 cups of boiling water. The boiling water will change the chemical composition of baking soda, making it more alkaline. Repeat a few times until the drain is clear.

## AVOID AIR FRESHNERS WITH HOUSEPLANTS

Commercial air fresheners work by masking smells and coating the nasal passages with chemicals that diminish the sense of smell by deadening the nerves. In addition, they also pollute the air. Houseplants act as natural air filters, so invest in a few and place them in areas such as the bathroom where they can counter unpleasant odors.

## YOUR EVERYDAY BATHROOM SPRAY

Make your own air freshener for the bathroom by filling a spray bottle with about 3 ounces water and 10 drops of neroli oil, which is renowned for its warm and relaxing qualities.

## HOMEMADE POTPOURRI

Make your own potpourri from mixed herbs such as peppermint and cloves, or sprinkle baking soda into a small basket or bowl to absorb smells in the bathroom.

# STRIKING IDEA FOR SMELLS

For a simple and instant idea to remove unpleasant smells in bathrooms, strike a match and blow it out. The sulfur released will clear the air.

# ARE THE MIRRORS FOGGED?

Reduce fogging in your bathroom by wiping mirrors with dishwashing liquid. Buff up vigorously with a cloth. A little shaving cream dabbed on the mirror works well also.

## Who Knew?

Speaking of mirrors, did you know that chimpanzees are the only animals other than humans to recognize themselves in a mirror?

## BECAUSE SOAP SLIME IS DISGUSTING...

...we offer this simple formula for ridding your bathroom of it. Wash slimy soap dishes by soaking them in 4 oz. of washing soda crystals dissolved in 6 pints of very hot water. Scrub with a toothbrush, rinse, and dry. Also, keep a sponge on your soap dish, and let the bar of soap rest on it, which will soak up any watery soap and prevent the mess from occurring in the first place. Just use the soapy sponge to wipe out the bathtub.

## MORE WAYS TO RID THE BATHROOM OF FOG

If you don't want to use dishwashing liquid on your mirror, eliminate fogging by wiping down your mirror with this solution and it will be shiny and fog-free: Mix 1 cup of white vinegar and 5 drops of eucalyptus oil in a spray bottle, spray on to the mirror, then wipe with a clean cloth.

## MIX YOUR OWN BATH OIL

Many bath oils that claim to contain natural products actually contain chemical compounds that have been designed to mimic the smell of herbs and fragrances. Instead of wasting your money on artificial smells, why not mix your own with your favorite essential oils? Try a mix of 3 drops of rosewood oil, 2 drops of sandalwood oil, 2 drops of clary sage oil, 1 drop of rose oil, 1 drop of chamomile, and 1 drop of marjoram oil. Add to the bath water.

## OATMEAL BATH

If you have irritated or itchy skin, try this oatmeal bath. Grind 2 cups of rolled oats into a fine powder and add to a bathful of warm water along with 10 drops of lavender oil. After soaking for up to 30 minutes, pat skin dry without rinsing.

## WE KNOW IT'S NOT A BATHROOM TIP, BUT SPEAKING OF OATMEAL...

Believe it or not, oatmeal can be very effective at relieving arthritis pain. Just mix two cups of oatmeal with one cup of water, warm in the microwave, and apply to the affected area.

## STRESS FREE BATH TIME

Make bath time a de-stressing experience with natural ingredients. Add 2 cups of Epsom salts as you run your bath. Then when the tub is full, add 5 drops each of lavender and sandalwood oils, and 2 drops of ylang ylang oil and stir into the water.

# BATH MILK

This bath milk is great to use in the bath before going to bed.

   1 cup powdered milk

   1 tablespoon almond oil

   lavender, marjoram and
   benzoin oils

Mix the powdered milk and almond oil, with 4 drops of lavender oil, 3 drops of marjoram oil, and 2 drops of benzoin oil. Add to the running water.

## CITRUS FRESH

It's easy to make a wonderful citrus bath. Simply zest the rind of an orange, lemon, lime, grapefruit, and tangerine. Blend all the peel until fine, adding in a cup or two of the fruits' juices. Pour as much of the mix as you want under running bath water.

## HERBAL SOAK FOR COLDS

Crush 2 teaspoons each of dried lavender and dried rosemary, along with 1 teaspoon each of powdered ginger and dried eucalyptus. Put the herbs in the middle of a handkerchief or cloth and tie the ends. Hang the bag under the faucet while running the bath.

## BATH SALTS

Why buy bath salts when you can make your own this easily?

   1 cup instant powered milk

   1 cup baking soda

   2 tablespoons cornstarch

   1 tablespoon cream of tartar

   1 tablespoon cinnamon

Mix ingredients together and store in an airtight container. Add to your bath as needed.

## LEMON UPLIFT

Mix 20 drops each of lemon and tangerine oils with 25 drops each of neroli and lavender oils and add to bath as needed. This can also be used in an oil diffuser in the bathroom.

## THERAPEUTIC EPSOM SALTS

Epsom salt has wonderful, purifying properties, and is wonderful on your skin.

 6 cups Epsom salts

 2 cups baking soda

 1 cup sea salt

Mix all ingredients, and shake to blend. Store in an airtight container, and add a handful to your bath as desired. Afterwards, make sure your moisturize your skin.

## VANILLA BATH

Vanilla had calming properties which make it a terrific addition to your bathwater.

 1 cup sunflower oil

 ½ cup castile soap

 1 tablespoon real vanilla extract

 ¼ cup honey

Mix together all ingredients.Use ¼ of a cupful per bath.

## MAKE YOUR OWN TALC

Try this natural alternative to talcum powder.

 1 cup powdered arrowroot

 1 cup cornstarch

 ¼ cup baking soda

 vanilla beans (optional)

 rose petals (optional)

Mix powdered arrowroot, cornstarch, cornstarch, and baking soda. Pour into an airtight container. To add fragrance, add either a few vanilla beans or a cup of rose petals.

# 6

# BEDROOM

The bedroom is the one place we all spend the majority of our lives. Follow these tips to keep it warm, wonderful, and chemical free.

## SLEEP NATURALLY

Don't reach for the sleeping pills next time you're having trouble dropping off—not only can you become reliant on using them to get to sleep, but many also give you a hangover the next day. Try natural sleep enhancers such as lavender essential oil and chamomile tea.

## THE SALT SOLUTION

Here's another natural way to get to sleep without pills: At bedtime drink a glass of water, then let a pinch of salt dissolve on your tongue. (Just make sure the salt doesn't touch the roof of your mouth). Studies show the combination of salt and water can induce a deep sleep.

## FUTONS

A futon is a great choice for a bed if you are short of space. When shopping for one, remember to choose a futon with a removable cover for washing. To spot clean, isolate any spills immediately by tying with a rubber band then clean with water or a mild soapy solution. Make sure you air out futons regularly and turn weekly to prevent the mattress compacting.

## BREAKFAST IN BED

Mop up stains and spills on duvets or quilts at once to avoid soaking through to the filling. If the casing is stained, ease the filling away from that area. Tie off with an elastic band or string. Sponge first with cold water, and then go over the area with mild detergent.

## CLEANING YOUR BEDROOM

When vacuuming your bedroom, give it a fragrance to aid sleep by mixing 1 cup of baking soda with a few drops of lavender oil or even a handful of fresh lavender if you grow it in your garden. Sprinkle over the bedroom carpet, leave for an hour, and the vacuum up.

## SWEET DREAMS

For deep and restful sleep, spray your pillowcases and sheets with lavender spray made by adding a few drops of lavender oil to a spray bottle of water.

## BLANKET IN-STRUCTION

Freshen up blankets (including electric ones) by sprinkling them with a little baking soda, which will absorb odors. Brush away the excess with a clothes brush.

## STAINED MATTRESS

Sponge the mattress with a solution of 1 tablespoon of borax dissolved in a little hot water and added to 2 cups of water. Then sponge again with warm water. Allow to dry thoroughly.

# SATIN

Clean satin pillows with the soft brush attachment of the vacuum cleaner. Treat any greasy stains with a sprinkling of flour or baking soda, leave overnight, and then brush off the excess.

## WET BED

Soak up as much excess as possible, then mix 1 cup of baking soda with 3 drops eucalyptus oil or tea tree oil and liberally sprinkle over the wet area. Leave to dry, in the sun if possible, and then vacuum the powder away. The baking soda will absorb the fluid and deodorize at the same time. You may have to repeat the process.

## Who Knew?

Alpine, N.J. has the distinction of having the most bedrooms per home of any city in the United States. On average, each home there has 6.71 bedrooms.

## MOTHS

To prevent moths, place horse chestnuts in cupboards and closets. They are easy to find on the Internet and aren't expensive. Storing out-of-season clothes in airtight bags or plastic containers is another great way to keep away moths.

## WARD OFF MOTHS

Moths are attracted to wool, mohair, and angora, and also to stains on these clothes. Make sure clothes are clean before storing. Moths are destroyed by laundering, air, and sunlight, so always hang your clothes outside before storing if possible. For added protection, you can add a few drops of eucalyptus oil to the final rinse, when your washing your wool clothes, and soak for 30 minutes. You can also hang a bag of herbs such as eucalyptus, lavender, or peppermint in your closet to ward them off.

# CEDAR FOR MOTHS

Cedar is also extremely good at keeping moths at bay, so consider buying cedar shavings for closets or drawers. You can also try cedar blocks, which can be sanded once in a while to renew their scent.

## Who Knew?

Over 140,000 different types of moths have been discovered worldwide.

# DRAWER LINERS

Don't buy scented drawer liners from the store. Make your own simply by using left over gift wrap or brown paper, and spraying it with your favorite essential oils. You can also add bunches of lavender. Scented sachets are especially good in your lingerie drawer.

## FRESH DRAWERS

Instead of using scented sheets which contains a host of unwanted chemicals on your clothes, use aromatherapy bags in drawers to freshen clothes up as they are being stored, and make them smell sweet and fresh. If you find that lavender is too strong, try dried sage, thyme, or marjoram instead.

## CITRUS CLOSET AIR FRESHENER

Poking whole cloves into an orange until it is nearly covered can make a simple and effective air freshener. Then, simply tie a ribbon or piece of string around the orange and hang up it in your closet.

## SCENTED SACHETS

If your shoes are in need of freshening up, create a sachet by placing 2 or 3 teaspoons of baking soda in the middle of a circle of cotton. Secure with a rubber band and place a sachet in each shoe overnight. You could also add a few drops of your favorite essential oil. Of course, our favorite way to freshen stinky sneakers is to place them in a plastic bag, and keep in the freezer overnight. In the morning, the smell will be gone!

## FRESHEN DRAWERS

Wash wooden drawers in warm soapy water. For laminated plastic, use 1 ounce of distilled white vinegar mixed with 1¾ pints of warm water. Air dry if possible or wipe with a cloth.

## SILVERFISH, PERHAPS THE MOST DIGUSTING INSECT EVER CREATED

If you have silverfish in your bedroom, place whole cloves in closets and drawers. In addition, you can sprinkle Epson salts where you find the pests also.

## HAIRBRUSH

Keep hairbrushes clean by soaking them every so often in a bowl of warm, soapy water with ¼ of a cup of baking soda added. Soak for 30 minutes and scrub with a nailbrush if needed before rinsing.

## ON THE CASE

If your suitcase or trunk has a musty smell after being stored away, place an open tin of clay cat litter inside. Close and leave it overnight. By the morning, the unpleasant odors should be gone.

# 7

# WINDOWS & OUTSIDE SPACES

There are so many effective, natural ways to clean your windows, and rid your garden of pests, that you'll never need to buy chemical-laden products again. Here are some of our favorites.

## A LOSING STREAK

Sometimes streaky windows are caused by a build up of wax from commercial cleaning products. Use this cleaner first before switching to one of the other stronger recipes which follow.

   ½ cup isopropyl rubbing alcohol

   ¼ teaspoon natural dishwashing soap

   water

Mix the rubbing alcohol with ½ cup of warm water, and the natural dishwashing soap in a spray bottle and shake well. Spray onto windows and wipe with a clean, lint-free cloth.

## WONDERFUL LEMON OIL GLASS CLEANER

Club soda and water is the easiest way to clean windows, but if they're really dirty, try this wonderful lemon cleaner.

   ⅓ cup distilled white vinegar

   lemon oil

   water

   natural dishwashing soap

Mix ⅔ of a cup of water with the distilled white vinegar, and add just 2 drops of lemon oil. Shake well and spray. Wipe glass clean with a clean, lint-free cloth, or a crumpled newspaper. If your windows are especially dirty, try adding ¼ of a teaspoon of natural dishwashing soap to the mixture.

## FRESH LEMON GLASS CLEANER

This is a terrific formula for greasy windows. Unlike the "Wonderful Lemon Oil Cleaner," this won't keep as well so refrigerate after use.

> 2 teaspoons freshly squeezed and
>   strained lemon juice
>
> purified water

Add the freshly squeezed and strained lemon juice to 16 fl. oz. of water (purified is best). Be sure to strain, so you don't get the lemon bits all over your glass. Apply with a soft cloth, and dry with a clean cloth or crumpled newspaper.

## HEAVY-DUTY WINDOW CLEANER

> 1 cup distilled white vinegar
>
> peppermint essential oil
>
> liquid castile soap
>
> water

In a bucket mix 8 cups of hot water with the vinegar, and 8 drops of mint essential oil. Use a sponge to apply to windows, starting from the top. Wipe away with a clean cloth or the squeegee blade, then wipe over again with a clean damp cloth. Remove last traces of dampness with a chamois. If windows are particularly dirty, add 1 tablespoon of liquid castile soap to the mix for extra power to cut through the grime.

# SIMPLE GLASS CLEANER

For quick and easy general glass cleaning, use a solution of equal parts of vinegar and water. Spray onto the glass and wipe clean.

# FLY SPOTS

If you have fly spots on glass or mirrors, try making some tea, letting it cool, and then apply to the glass with a soft, clean cloth. Fly spots should come off easily.

# PAINT SPOTS

To remove paint spots from glass, try using a razor blade for any larger paint spots. Tiny paint spots can be removed by putting a little baking soda onto a clean nylon-backed sponge. Use the back of the sponge to rub the little dots off.

## SOAP-ONLY WINDOW CLEANER

When cleaning your windows outside, try adding one squirt of natural dishwashing liquid soap to a bucket of water. If you use any more you will get soap residue on your windows. Any residue can be removed using a vinegar rinse. Use newspaper to dry.

## GLEAMING GLASS

For glass that stays clean and static-free, add 1 tablespoon of corn flour to about 2 pints of lukewarm water. Wet a cloth, squeeze away excess water, and wipe down the glass. Because the rag is less static, dust and debris build up less frequently.

## PRISTINE PLASTIC

Avoid using any cleaners containing ammonia on plastic windows as it leaves the surface permanently cloudy. Instead, use a handful of pure soap flakes mixed with 1 tablespoon of washing soda and 1 pint of water.

## ARE YOUR PLASTIC SHUTTERS GRIMY?

Then try this. Mix 7 ounces of vinegar to 5 pints of water. Open the window to its fullest extent so that the slats are perpendicular with the window frame. Dip a thick white cotton sock in the solution, wring, and place over your hand like a mitten. Starting at the top, clean the slats on both sides. Use the other clean dry sock to dry in the same manner.

## PROTECT YOUR WOODEN SHUTTERS

Clean wood shutters with linseed oil. Dampen a cloth with boiled linseed oil that has cooled and rub into the wood for great looking shutters.

### Who Knew?

Whether you clean your windows with crumpled newspaper or clean cloths, always dry the inside of your windows with vertical strokes, and the outside with horizontal strokes. That way, if there are streaks, you'll know what side to clean.

# SHADY BUSINESS

The first sunny day of spring is a great day to clean your windows, right? Wrong. Strong sunlight can cause any window cleaners to dry before you can work it off and this may cause streaks. Try cleaning your windows out of the full glare of the sun.

## ALUMINUM FRAMES

Window and door frames made of aluminum have a tough coating, but they're not so tough that abrasive cleaners won't scratch the coating. To prevent that, avoid any abrasive cleanser, and use a smooth cloth and a bowl of hot water and dishwashing liquid soap when cleaning. Then make sure you dry thoroughly afterwards.

## LEAD AND STAINED GLASS

Leaded and stained glass windows require extra care. Wash the panes individually with warm water and a clean cloth. Make sure you don't use too much force or you can actually bend them. Never wash with household glass cleaners, vinegar, lemon, ammonia, or anything with an abrasive action.

## ALUMINUM AND VINYL BLINDS

Don't use ammonia or any other harsh abrasive or cleaner on aluminum or vinyl blinds. Instead, wash with water and a little dishwashing liquid soap, and then rinse off with clean water. Of course, the easiest way to clean your blinds is to simply take them down and wash in the shower or tub.

## DO YOU CUT OFF THE CRUSTS?

You can clean Venetian or slatted blinds with crusts of fresh bread. Just hold the crusts against each slat as you run them along the length of the blind. An old paintbrush will also do the same job, or use the brush attachment on your vacuum cleaner.

# THE CASE OF THE STICKY KEYS

If your key keeps sticking in your lock, work a pencil over the grooves in the key and gently inside the keyhole, too. (Just be careful not to break off the tip of the pencil inside the lock.) Then, work the lock with the key. The graphite in the pencil acts to lubricate the two components.

# PAINTED DOORS

Most marks and smudges on painted doors will come away if you wipe them down with either vinegar or baking soda on a damp clean cloth.

## CREAKING DOORS?

Use a pencil to go over the joints in your hinges. The graphite in the pencil lubricates the hinges without corroding them. Being dry, graphite won't promote rust. Afterwards, work the door back and forth a few times and repeat the process.

## BRASS DOOR FITTINGS

Apply white, non-gel toothpaste on a soft cloth to door fittings, and then rub firmly on the brass. Use a fresh cloth to wipe clean. For lacquered brass door fittings, protect with a light coating of olive or lemon oil.

### Who Knew?

Throw away the turpentine, my friends, when you need to get paint off your hands. Instead, reach for the olive oil, which will do the same job—it just won't harm your skin or the environment in the process.

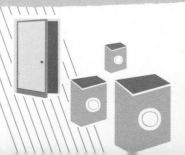

## DO YOU COOK WITH A PLATE ON YOUR BARBECUE GRILL?

If you do, try this simple way to clean it up. While the plate is still hot after cooking, sprinkle it liberally with salt to absorb all the grease. Then, once it is dry, simply brush the salt deposits away. If you have a barbecue plate that needs cleaning before you can cook on it, give it a scrub with salt water. Use a soft brush, and wipe the surface dry with a cloth. Smear the surface with a little vegetable or linseed oil to prevent it from rusting.

## ALL THE NEWS THAT'S FIT TO CLEAN

A great way to clean your barbeque grill is with wet newspaper. After cooking, just place it on a warm grill for 1 hour, spray with a mixture of water and white vinegar, and close the lid. You'll be amazed how easy the grime then comes off!

## ALTERNATIVE TO DISINFECTANT

Try this natural alternative for wiping down garage floors or rinsing out outside garbage cans. To a nearly full bottle of distilled white vinegar, add 50 drops of tea tree oil and shake well. Add the mixture to a bucket of hot water, and clean away.

# OIL LEAK

If you spill oil or anti-freeze on your garage floor, sprinkle a layer of clean cat litter over the area. Leave it for a few hours then sweep up and throw away. Then clean the floor with a citrus cleaning product to cut through any remaining grease.

# ICE BREAKER, WITHOUT THE SALT

When it's freezing and rainy or snowy outside, don't reach for the rock salt. It's filled with chemicals, and if you sprinkle it on your steps and landing outside the front door, it gets tracked inside your home. Instead, mix a solution of a gallon of hot water and two tablespoons of natural dishwashing liquid, and pour it all over steps. The dishwashing liquid has properties that inhibit freezing, so your steps should not ice up.

## CEMENT

To clean cement stains from tools, floors, or outside surfaces, scrub with a solution made with ¼ of a cup of borax dissolved in ½ a cup of hot water, and then added to 2 cups of water. Just apply, let it sit for a while, and then scrub and hose down.

## STONE STEPS

Sweep stone steps regularly to remove leaves and twigs, or they can stain and the steps become covered in mold. Once a year, squirt a little natural dishwashing liquid soap on the steps, spray on some water, and take a stiff-bristled brush to it. Rinse with a garden hose. Treat stone patios in the same way.

### Who Knew?

The rock salt commonly used to salt icy sidewalks and steps is so filled with corrosive chemicals, it can actually eat through cement, leaving your walk pockmarked.

## ROOT OF THE PROBLEM

Don't use weed killer in your garden. It might appear to be the quick and easy option but could make your weeds grow back stronger. Weeding by hand is very effective as it weakens the weed at the root. Pull up weeds before they go to seed and self-spread, and make sure you get the whole weed including the root.

## MULCH FOR WEEDS

Instead of weed killer, use mulch between flowers to prevent weeds getting a hold in the first place. For really hardy weeds that grow through the mulch, use flax matting, cardboard, or weed-reducing matting.

## TABLE SALT TO THE RESCUE

If you're plagued by dandelions and reticent to use chemicals in the garden, consider this tried and true method: dig out the offending plant, and drop a little salt in the hole. The dandelions won't come back.

# INSECT HAVEN

Try to leave an area of dead wood in your garden as an insect haven where natural insect life is encouraged to develop. It doesn't have to be huge—a few broken logs will do and you'll soon reap the wildlife benefits in your garden.

# NATURAL WEED KILLER

Instead of commercial weed killer in your garden, squirt springtime weeds with lemon juice or vinegar or alternatively carefully scald them with boiling water. Repeat as necessary.

# IT'S NOT JUST FOR SALAD DRESSING

Olive oil is a terrific moisturizer for rubber hoses and gaskets. Just apply it car door seals and gaskets, garden hoses—anything rubber that tends to crack over time.

## POTATOES

Potatoes hold onto toxins if pesticides are used. Buy organic or, if you want to protect your homegrown potatoes from flea beetles, try planting your potatoes with collard greens. Never add lime to the soil before planting potatoes.

## AND KEEP A BAG HANDY, TOO, JUST IN CASE

A terrific way to avoid carsickness is to open the car's window, and place a few drops of peppermint essential oil on a tissue. Inhale the scent deeply, and the nauseousness should pass.

## CLEAN SEEDS

Seeds often carry diseases, so they should be treated before being planted. You can lessen the possibility of disease by using the following wash for them: In a bowl mix 1 tablespoon of apple cider vinegar and 1 quart of water. Put the seeds on a piece of clean cheesecloth and tie the ends to make a bag. Dip the bag into the bowl several times then remove seeds and spread out to allow to dry thoroughly.

## GARDEN FURNITURE

To clean plastic garden furniture of marks and stains, try using hot soapy water. If the stains are tough, dissolve 1 cup of washing soda in a bucket of hot water and scrub the stains with this solution using a brush or a scourer. Store plastic garden furniture inside over the winter to avoid it getting stained.

## DO YOU SMELL LIKE A SKUNK?

If you get sprayed by a skunk, you won't have to throw out your stinky clothes if you follow this simple formula: Into a gallon of water, add one pint of hydrogen peroxide, one small box of baking soda, and a squirt of any natural dishwashing liquid. Soak your clothes for an hour, and the smell should be gone. Launder as usual. Be aware that this recipe loses its effectiveness in about an hour, so use it as soon as you mix it up.

# FOR THE CLEANEST GARDEN TOOLS

Always keep a bucket of coarse sand dampened with mineral oil for cleaning your garden tools. When you've finished using your tools, just hose off the dirt, and put the blades into the sand a few times. The tools will be cleaned, oiled...and ready to use again.

# 8

# CLOTHING STAINS

The most important thing to remember when treating stains on clothing is to *act fast*. You need to get to stains as soon as possible, because virtually every stain is harder to remove when it is allowed to sit untreated. You'll also need to know what fabric you're treating, and how to treat the stain—so read this chapter carefully. We've arranged it alphabetically by stain, so it's easy to use. The good news is, with all the natural products you probably have on hand, the next time your kid spills grape juice on your pants, you'll be ready. Good luck!

# BABY FORMULA

To remove baby formula from clothes, soak the affected area in vinegar for a couple of hours before washing in lukewarm water.

## ACID

Mop up the spill quickly and then soak the area in cold water. To neutralize the acid, apply a paste of baking soda and water. When the paste is dry, brush away before sponging down with water.

## ALCOHOL

If you are in a restaurant, use club soda to soak the stain, then blot dry with napkins. If you're at home, try soaking the item in a bucket of cold water, with ½ a cup of vinegar added to it. After soaking for a couple of hours, wash as usual. For a particularly stubborn stain, soak in a weak borax solution: 1 tablespoon of borax dissolved in a little hot water and added to a bucket of cool water. Note: red wine stains are a different kind of animal; the formulas for removing those stains are found on pg. 143 in this chapter.

## BABY SPIT UP

When the stain is fresh, wipe away excess and run cold water through the fabric to remove all traces. If this is not possible to do so immediately, then dab the area with club soda. If the stain has dried, soak the affected area in white vinegar before washing as usual.

## BALLPOINT PEN

Place a rolled-up towel or cloth behind the stained area and dab at the stain with eucalyptus oil until it disappears.

## BARBECUE SAUCE

Flush immediately with cold running water, and then soak in a solution of 1 cup of white vinegar in a bucket of water for 30 minutes before washing as usual. If the stain persists, apply a paste of cream of tartar and water. Let the paste dry, then launder as usual.

### Who Knew?

It's important never to rub a fresh stain with a bar of soap. Many stains can get set further when treated with soap.

## BEETS

If possible, run cold water through the stain to remove as much of it as possible, or soak the item in milk for a few hours before washing as usual. For a more stubborn stain, apply a paste of cream of tartar and water, let it dry, and then wash as usual.

## BERRIES

Run cold water through the stain to remove as much stain as possible. Then try either dabbing the affected area with lemon juice or applying a paste of cream of tartar and water and allow to dry. Follow up either treatment by washing the garment as usual, using lukewarm water. If the stain is old, apply either cream of tartar paste or a little glycerin, and leave for a couple of hours before washing as usual.

## BIRD DROPPINGS

This is one of the rare cases when it's better to let the stain set before removing it. For best results, let the droppings dry before scraping them away. Then sponge the stained area with a solution of 2 tablespoons of vinegar in ½ a cup of water.

## BLOOD

Never use hot water on a bloodstain. If possible, run cold water through the stained area, then soak in cold water for several hours before washing as usual using lukewarm water. For a more stubborn stain, mix cornstarch, baking soda, and a little water into a spreadable paste and apply, then allow to dry and brush away. In the case of a very small bloodstain, saliva will break it down. Spit on the stain, as disgusting as that sounds, wait for a few minutes, and then wash the garment as usual. If the blood has dried on the fabric, apply a paste of borax and water. Once the paste has dried, brush it away, and then wash the item as usual.

## BURN MARKS

If the fabric is white, rub lemon juice into the mark, and leave the item to dry in the sun. Otherwise, soak in a solution of 2 tablespoons of borax dissolved in a little hot water and then added to 2 cups of water. Soak until the mark fades, and then wash as usual.

## BUBBLE GUM

Place the affected item in a plastic bag, and leave in the freezer for a couple of hours, or use an ice cube to harden the gum. Then use a knife to scrape the gum gently off the fabric. To get the last fragments of gum out, either soak the garment in white vinegar or dab the stain with eucalyptus oil. Then wash the garment as normal. By the way, did you know that the easiest way to remove bubble gum from a kid's hair is by working peanut butter through it?

## CEMENT

To remove cement from clothing, soak in a mixture made by adding 1 tablespoon of salt and 1 cup of white vinegar to a bucket of water. Then wash as usual.

## CHOCOLATE

Try soaking the stain in milk before washing as usual. You can also dab at the stain with a cloth dipped in a solution of 1 tablespoon of vinegar and ½ a cup of water, then wash in lukewarm water.

## COFFEE

Run cold water through the affected area and then apply a paste made with borax and water. Leave for an hour before washing as usual. Alternatively, mix egg yolk with lukewarm water and rub onto the stain, then wash as normal.

## ANOTHER GREAT COFFEE STAIN SOLUTION

To remove coffee stains from a favorite garment, stretch the garment over a bowl, cover the stain with salt, and pour boiling water over the stain from a height of one to two feet. (The gravity helps). Of course, always test first that the garment can withstand hot water (unlike, say, cashmere).

## COLLARS

To treat ring around the collar, apply a paste of cream of tartar and water. Leave to dry, then wash as usual. Another solution is to try a paste of liquid dishwashing soap and baking soda. Finally, in a pinch, a piece of white chalk does the trick.

## COSMETICS

Most cosmetic stains will come away if you dab at them with a solution of 1 tablespoon of borax dissolved in a little hot water and added to ½ a cup of water. You could also try applying a paste of cream of tartar and water. Leave to dry, and then wash as usual.

## CRAYONS

Start by scraping the stain with a butter knife to remove as much crayon as possible. Then, work some non-gel toothpaste into the stain, and it should lift it out. Wash as usual after the treatment.

## CURRY

Dissolve ¼ of a cup of borax in ½ a cup of hot water. Add to a bucket of water, and soak stained fabric before washing as usual.

## DEODORANT

Deodorant can leave dark stains on fabric in the area under the arms. There are several options to pre-treat before washing the garment as normal. Soak in either white vinegar or in a bucket of water to which you've added a solution of ¼ of a cup of borax dissolved in hot water. Another solution is to apply a paste of baking soda and water, and leave for a few hours.

## EGG

Do not use hot water to remove egg stains: the heat will cook the egg and make it harder to remove. Wash away excess, then soak the item in a bucket of cold water with ¼ of a cup of salt added.

## FELT

Small areas of staining on felt will come away if you rub lightly with fine sandpaper.

## FISH

For clothing stained with fish slime, flush with cold water as soon as possible, then soak overnight in a solution of ½ a cup of vinegar in a bucket of cold water. Finally, wash as usual.

## FOOD

If the specific food stain is not listed here, start by sponging with a solution of white vinegar and a little liquid soap. This may be enough to remove all signs of the stain on the fabric. If not, try cream of tartar mixed with a little water to a paste. Apply to the fabric, leave to dry, and then wash as normal.

## FRUIT STAINS I

Sprinkle club soda over the stained area and blot up the liquid. Then, sponge with a solution of 1 tablespoon of borax and 1 cup of hot water, or soak in ¼ of a cup of borax in a bucket of hot water, until the stain is removed. Wash as usual.

## FRUIT STAINS II

Another method for removing fruit stains is to sprinkle some salt on the garment, and then rinse it in cold water. Follow by washing in warm water with a natural liquid detergent. If the stain is still there, apply a little hydrogen peroxide.

# GASOLINE ODOR

Nothing stinks on your clothes like gasoline! To remove the odor, place the offending clothes in a bucket of cold water, and add a can of cola and a cup of baking soda. Soak overnight, then line dry outside if possible. If there is still any odor left, just wash as usual and it should be gone.

## GLUE

Soak the affected area in warm vinegar for about 10 minutes. Rinse away the residue and wash as normal. Eucalyptus oil will also effectively remove glue: drop a little onto a soft clean cloth and dab at the affected area until the glue comes away.

## GRASS STAINS I

For grass stains on fabric, soak the stained area in white vinegar and then wash in water as hot as possible for that particular fabric. Alternatively, wet the stain with cold water and rub on cream of tartar. Then rub in equal measures of vegetable glycerin and liquid dishwashing soap. Rinse off and wash as normal.

## GRASS STAINS II

Toothpaste, toothpaste, toothpaste. (The non-gel type). Need we say more?

## GREASE

It may be enough to sprinkle the spot with flour or cornstarch, and leave it for a while to absorb the grease. Shake away the flour and wash the garment as usual. Alternatively, run very hot water through the stain if possible, and apply eucalyptus oil to absorb the grease. Then wash as usual.

## GREASE (REALLY TOUGH STAINS)

If the formula above doesn't work, try soaking the grease stain with rubbing alcohol, then blotting with a clean white cloth. If it's still there, rub in some natural laundry detergent with a soft toothbrush, and put garment in a bucket of water to which you've added a can of cola. If that doesn't work…you have our condolences.

## GREASE ON SUEDE

Get rid of greasy marks on suede by dipping a toothbrush in vinegar and gently brushing it over the grease spot.

## HAIR DYE

Flush with cold water before soaking in a solution of ¼ of a cup of borax dissolved in ½ a cup of hot water that had been added to a bucket of cold water. Then wash as normal.

## HONEY

Flush with warm water to wash away residue. If a stain remains, apply a paste of borax and water. Leave to dry, and then wash as usual.

## INK

Try soaking the stained area in milk for a few hours and then wash as usual. You can also dab vegetable oil onto the area so that the ink is thinned out, then blot it away with a cloth. Repeat until the stain begins to fade, and then wash as usual. If you get ink on your hands, rub vegetable oil onto your fingers, wiping away the ink with a cloth. Then wash your hands in warm water.

## JAM, JELLY AND MARMALADE

For jam, jelly or marmalade stains, wipe off the surplus, and then sponge with a cloth moistened in a warm water and natural dishwashing liquid solution. If the mark persists, rub on a little borax powder, leave for a few minutes, sponge clean, and then wash as normal.

## LACE

White lace can become yellowed with age. To remove the yellow staining, soak the lace for a couple of hours in a solution of 1 tablespoon of borax dissolved in a little hot water before adding to 4 cups of water. Then wash with a mild soap, and rinse well. Dry in the sun if possible.

## LINEN

Linen can become quite yellowed with age. To restore whiteness and remove yellow stains, sponge with a solution of borax and lemon juice. Alternatively, try pressing borax powder into the stained area on half a lemon, making sure that the area is well moistened. Leave to dry, and then wash as usual.

## LIPSTICK

Eucalyptus oil will remove lipstick from fabric. Simply add a few drops to a cloth and dab at the stain until it disappears. Rubbing either petroleum jelly or glycerin gently into the stain before washing is also effective, but can be oily.

## MAKEUP

To remove makeup stains, rub shampoo or natural liquid dish detergent into the stain. Then, launder as usual.

# LEATHER

The best way we know of to clean leather is to beat an egg white until stiff, and then rub it into the leather with a cloth. Repeat as needed until the stain is totally removed. If gum has become stuck to the leather, remove it by rubbing a plastic bag full of ice cubes over it to harden the gum, then remove. If there is any residual, point a hair dryer set on warm towards the gum, then rub it clean with a clean cloth once it softens.

## MASCARA

To clean mascara marks from clothing, dab with
eucalyptus oil on a soft cloth.

## MEDICINE, LIQUID

Flush the area immediately with cold water, then
apply a paste of borax and water for a few hours
before washing as usual. Or, dab the stain with half a
cut lemon dipped in salt, leave to dry, and then wash
as usual.

## MILDEW

Rub the stain with a mix of buttermilk and salt and
then wash in the hottest water the fabric will allow.
If your fabric is white, hang outside to use the sun's
rays to bleach the fabric.

## MILDEW IN SWIMSUITS

Soak the swimsuit in warm soapy water and ½ cup
of borax, and ¼ cup of hydrogen peroxide. With
a clean cloth, gently rub the stain until it is gone.
Launder the garment and usual, and dry in the sun
if possible.

## MILK

Soak the item in cold water and rub with a little liquid dishwashing soap if needed before washing as usual.

## MOLD

Sometimes mold or mildew will come away simply with a good brush. Use a toothbrush and rub briskly over the affected area. Then, wash in warm water. You can also soak the fabric overnight in a solution of ½ a cup of vinegar and 1 tablespoon of salt. Then wash in warm water, and dry in the fresh air.

## MOTHBALL ODOR

To get rid of that funky mothball smell, hang your garments outside in the fresh air, if at all possible, for a full day. Afterwards, launder the clothing as usual, adding a cup of white vinegar to your detergent. Line dry afterwards, and do not use put your garments in the clothes dryer until you are certain the mothball smell is gone.

## MUD

For mud on clothing, small dry patches may brush off. Otherwise rinse under a cold running faucet, and then apply a paste of cream of tartar and water. Leave to dry, and then wash as usual.

**Who Knew?**

You can refresh your black clothes by adding two cups of strong coffee to your washing machine during the final rinse. It should help return your black clothes to their original color.

## MULBERRIES

To remove the deep red stain of fresh mulberries, use unripe, green mulberries. Rub them into the stain, and then wash fabric as usual.

## NAIL POLISH

The best way to remove nail polish is with a commercially available organic nail polish remover. To remove nail polish from fabric, blot up as much as possible, and test the remover on an inconspicuous spot before using it to dab at the stain. Then wash as normal.

## NEWSPRINT

Dab glycerin on the area to loosen the print, and then sponge with a solution of ¼ of a cup of vinegar and 1 cup of water.

## NICOTINE

To remove nicotine from fabric, dab with eucalyptus oil on a clean cloth until the stain comes off and then wash as normal. You can also rub eucalyptus oil onto nicotine-stained fingers, as this will remove the stain. Then, wash your hands as normal with soap and water.

## NYLON

To treat yellowing stains on nylon, soak the affected item in a bucket of warm water with ¼ of a cup of baking soda added. Then wash as usual and allow to drip dry away from direct sunlight.

## PERFUME

Flush immediately with club soda, mopping up the liquid with a clean towel. If the stain persists, dab with glycerin and leave for two hours before either washing as usual or sponging away with warm water.

**Who Knew?**

When it doubt, try not-gel toothpaste: it really removes most stains—even grape juice!

## PERMANENT MARKER

Because these inks are meant to be permanent, they will understandably be difficult to remove. But you'll find that at least some of the stain will come away if you soak the fabric overnight in 1 cup of hot water with 2 tablespoons of borax added. Then wash as usual.

## PERSPIRATION

Perspiration marks will come away if you soak clothing in a solution made by adding 1 cup of baking soda to a bucket of warm water. Soak for a couple of hours before washing as usual. Also, warmed vinegar will do the trick: soak the affected area for 1 hour, and then wash as usual.

## PERSPIRATION II

Another natural way to remove perspiration stains from white shirts is to crush four aspirins into ½ cup of warm water, and apply to the stain. Soak for at least three hours, and launder as usual. If the stain is still there, well, you always need more polishing cloths, right?

## POLLEN

Clear plastic sticky tape lifts pollen away from fabric. After you have removed the pollen, wash as normal.

## RED WINE

Blot up as much liquid as possible. If you have any white wine handy, pour it over the stained fabric as soon as possible. Otherwise, douse with club soda. Wash the garment as normal. Alternatively, pour a thick layer of salt over the stained area, let it absorb the wine, then wash off.

## RED WINE II

Another way to remove red wine stains is to apply a mixture of dishwashing liquid and vinegar, which is safe on all washable fabrics. Or, if your fabric is shrink-proof, try this: add it to a pot containing enough milk to cover the stain and bring it to a boil. Then remove it from the heat, and let sit until the stain has disappeared.

## BECAUSE WE SPILL A LOT OF RED WINE, LET ME PRESENT " RED WINE III"

A fail-safe way to remove red wine stains (on garments you know won't shrink) is to stretch the stained garment over a bowl, cover it in salt, and pour boiling water over the stain from a height of one to two feet. And then switch to white wine.

## Who Knew?

Over the past several decades, many studies have been published in science journals which make the point that drinking red wine alcohol is associated with reduced mortality due to heart disease. Yippee.

# SAP

Dab eucalyptus oil onto the stained area until the sap is removed. Then wash as usual.

## RUST

Sprinkle the stained area with a generous heap of salt, and then rub in a few tablespoons of lemon juice. Place the garment in the sun, reapplying lemon juice whenever it dries out. Later, rinse the garment. Alternatively try saturating the rust stains with sour milk (milk mixed with a little vinegar or lemon juice) and rub with salt. Place the item in direct sunlight until dry, and then wash it; the rust stain should disappear.

## SCORCH MARKS

To remove iron scorch marks from colorfast clothing and fabrics, gently boil the scorched article in 1 cup of soap flakes and 4 pints of milk for 10 minutes. Then rinse thoroughly, allow to dry, and wash normally.

## Who Knew?

Blot, but never rub, a stain. Rubbing will make your stain grow, which you don't want to happen.

## SHINY PATCHES

The best way to remove shiny patches from your clothing is to avoid them altogether. Before ironing dark pants, for example, always turn the legs inside out, and you'll avoid shiny spots on the cuffs and pockets. Your dry cleaner is also a culprit. Make sure your remove any collar stays before sending your clothes out to be laundered.

## SHOE POLISH

Scrape off as much as possible, then dab with eucalyptus oil on a clean cloth, turning the cloth as polish comes away so you don't re-soil the area. You could also try glycerin, dabbed on in the same way, before washing the item as usual.

## SOFT DRINKS

Run cold water through the fabric as soon as possible after the spill, and then soak in a solution of ½ cup of white vinegar in a bucket of water to remove all traces of the soft drink. Wash as usual. Alternatively, spray club soda over the affected area, and dab at it with a clean cloth or napkin until all traces of the stain have been removed.

## SOOT

Use adhesive tape to remove as much of the soot as you can. Avoid rubbing—this will spread the stain. Dab with eucalyptus oil, leave for 1 hour, and then wash as usual. Avoid using hot water on stains of unknown origin. Hot water can set protein stains such as milk, egg, or blood.

## Who Knew?

After laundering stained fabrics, always check the garments to ensure the spots are gone before machine drying or ironing. Using your clothes dryer or iron will help set the stains, so beware.

## Who Knew?

If you know you want to treat a stain but don't have time to do so immediately, tie a knot in the leg or sleeve before tossing the garment into the hamper. That way, you'll remember to pretreat the stain before laundering.

## SOUP

The way you treat the stain will depend on the ingredients of the soup. However, club soda is a good general treatment. Spray the area with club soda, and use a towel to mop up the liquid. If a stain remains after this treatment, soak in, or sponge with, a solution made of ¼ of a cup of borax dissolved in ½ a cup of hot water and added to a bucket of water.

## SUEDE

Clean any marks from suede without using chemical sprays for suede by brushing with either a soft brush if a delicate fabric or a brush with harder bristles, if a more substantial item. Believe it or not, balled-up pantyhose also are effective at cleaning suede.

## SUNSCREEN

Soak the area in distilled white vinegar until the lotion comes away. Then sponge with water.

## SYRUP

Soak the fabric in a solution of ½ cup of vinegar and
½ cup of warm water until the syrup stain appears
to have dissolved. Then, wash as usual. Also, you can
add ¼ of a cup of borax to 2 cups of hot water, and
soak in this solution before washing as usual.

## TAR

Scrape gently to remove any excess. Soften with
glycerin solution, rub well in, and leave for about 1
hour. Dab with eucalyptus oil holding a towel or an
absorbent cloth behind the fabric.

## TEA

Rinse with cool water before applying a little lemon
or lime juice. Wash as usual. Alternatively, soak for a
couple of hours in a solution of 2 cups of water and
1 tablespoon of borax, first dissolved in a little hot
water. Then wash as usual.

## TOMATO

Here's a helpful tip for when you get a tomato sauce
stain on your favorite shirt: immediately apply a bit
of shaving cream to the stain, and dab with a damp,
warm sponge. Let it dry and launder as usual, and
your shirt should look good as new.

## TOMATO II

You can also try to remove tomato stains by soaking in a solution of 1 tablespoon of borax first dissolved in a little hot water and added to 2 cups of water before washing as normal.

## URINE

Clean up urine on clothes by soaking the garment in a solution of distilled white vinegar and water to deodorize and treat the stain. Then wash as normal.

## VOMIT

Clean off as much of the nasty mess as you can, and then soak the garment in a solution made with 1 tablespoon of borax dissolved in hot water, to which you've added 2 cups of water. After soaking, launder as normal.

## WAX

Place the garment in the freezer to harden the wax, and then scrape off as much as you can with a knife. You'll need a roll of brown paper or a brown paper bag. Put the brown paper on your ironing board, place the stained area of your garment over it, and then cover with more brown paper. With your iron on a low to medium setting, gently press on the stained area. You'll see the brown paper blotting up the wax. Move the paper around, both underneath and over the stained area, and keep pressing with the iron until no more wax is being blotted up. Then wash the garment as usual.

## ZINC CREAM

Zinc effectively prevents sunburn by protecting the skin, but zinc cream can often get onto clothing, especially when clothing is pulled over the head. For zinc cream smears, sponge with hot vinegar, and then wash the item as usual.

# YELLOWING STAINS

To treat white clothes with yellowing stains without using bleach, soak for a couple of hours in a solution of either ½ a cup of lemon juice or ½ a cup of white vinegar added to a bucket of warm water. Then wash as normal.

## Who Knew?

If your clothes are extra greasy, add a can of lemon-lime soda to your washing machine along with detergent. The citric acid in the soda breaks down the oil in the greasy clothes, and your wash will sparkle.

# 9

# LAUNDRY

Traditional laundry detergents contain phosphates, which are a major cause of water pollution in the United States. Do your part to go green in the laundry—it's the right thing to do and you'll save money, too.

# IN THE WASH

Some liquid fabric softeners contain ammonium chloride, which is poison for our environment. Try adding ½ a cup of white vinegar to your wash instead. It will keep clothes soft and doesn't leave any scent behind.

1/2 cup

## THE BEST WAY TO WASH CLOTHES

Soapnut is a natural product that contains saponin, a natural soap. It is a terrific way to wash your laundry. Just put 6 to 8 opened soapnut shells into an unbleached cotton bag (or a knotted sock), place in your washing machine, and wash on your usual cycle (ideally a cool wash cycle). If you want your laundry to have a fragrance, add a few drops of essential oil in the softener drawer. Your washing will come out fresh, clean, and soft. You can also re-use soapnut shells, getting 4 to 6 consecutive loads from one batch. Soapnuts are for sale online by many retailers.

## BOIL YOUR SOCKS

Avoid using bleach on your dirty white socks. Simply boil them for 30-45 minutes with a sliced lemon, and line dry for fantastic non-chemical, whiter-than-white results. For really nasty socks, soak for several hours in salty water as hot as is suitable for the sock material. Then wash as usual again with hot water.

## SILK

To clean silk, soak the garment in approximately 1 cup of pure soap mixed with 2 to 3 tablespoons of baking soda, then squeeze the garment gently, rinse well and roll up in a towel to remove excess water.

## NATURAL BLEACH

Instead of using bleach to remove food stains, try a natural solution instead. Add ½ a cup of washing soda to each wash load to whiten up your whites and brighten colors.

## WASHING BASICS

Wash heavily soiled, dirty items separately from slightly soiled items. This will help prevent fading and keep colors brighter.

## PRESOAK SPRAY

Try this effective spray for heavy stains on your clothing before washing.

> 1 tablespoon liquid castile soap
>
> 1 tablespoon glycerin
>
> 1 tablespoon borax
>
> hot water
>
> 6 drops tea tree essential oil

Dissolve the borax in 1 cup of hot water, and then add the other ingredients. Spray on stains for 2 minutes, then launder as usual.

# FRAGRANT CLOTHES

If it's just the delicious fragrance in fabric softeners that you're really after on your clothes, yet you'd love to get rid of the chemicals the softeners are made with, simply drop a few drops of your favorite essential oil into your wash instead. It does the trick, and does no harm.

# REFRESH CLOTHES

If your clothes need refreshing in the wash, but aren't really dirty, try this for removing perspiration. Add ¼ of a cup of baking soda and ¼ of a cup of borax instead of detergent as your washing machine is filling and run it just on the rinse cycle.

## HEAVILY SOILED LAUNDRY

If you have heavily soiled clothes or whites to wash, instead of simply adding more detergent to your washing machine or using a higher temperature washing cycle, try pre-soaking your clothes in a solution of baking soda and water. This will yield the same results, with much less energy waste and water pollution.

## CHECK OUT THE MAGNETIC WAY TO WASH CLOTHES

Wash your clothes the magnetic way—without detergent— by investing in a unique magnetic laundry ball. When agitated, the ball produces ionized oxygen, which reduces the surface tension of water and allows it to penetrate fabrics and release dirt. Laundry balls are hypoallergenic, and therefore are suitable for sensitive skin, and save water, too. What's more, they can be re-used hundreds of times. Get more information online by searching for "magnetic laundry balls."

## REMOVE RESIDUE AND SAVE MONEY

Detergents can sometimes leave residue on clothes. Use half the amount of detergent normally used and add 1 cup of distilled white vinegar to the final rinse water to avoid residues. Never add vinegar to any wash if you are using chlorine bleach because the combination is toxic.

## OXYGEN BLEACH

If you must use bleach, then use oxygen bleaches because these rely on hydrogen peroxide to whiten clothes rather than chlorine, and are gentler on fabric and better for the environment. Oxygen bleaches work best if you soak clothes in the bleach solution for 2 hours. Then wash the clothes at the highest temperature designed for that fabric.

## TEE SHIRT SMARTS

To slow down how quickly your tee shirts fade, always wash them inside out.

# BRIGHT COLORS

Keep colors bright by simply adding 1 tablespoon of distilled white vinegar to each load of laundry rather than paying for special detergent for colored clothes. You can also prevent brand new brightly colored clothes from bleeding over all your other laundry by soaking them in vinegar before the first wash.

# SOFTEN CLOTHES

Try adding ½ a cup of baking soda to your machine's rinse cycle for soft and deodorized clothes rather than using fabric conditioners containing chemicals.

## MAKE YOUR OWN DETERGENT

For a homemade washing soap, mix 1 cup of baking soda with 10 drops each of lavender and grapefruit oils, adding the oil drop by drop and mixing thoroughly. Add 1 cup of borax and 1 cup of powdered castile soap. Store in an airtight container and add half a cup to each load of washing.

## GENERAL STAIN REMOVER

Many types of stains can be removed with this stain remover if treated quickly. Mix 1 tablespoon of vegetable glycerin, 1 tablespoon of natural dishwashing soap, and ½ a cup of water. Store in a bottle and squirt onto the stain before washing as normal.

## WANT TO UNSHRINK A SWEATER?

Um, sorry, it can't be done, but there are a few things you can try: soak the sweater in a hair conditioner and water solution, and pull gently to reshape; lay flat to dry. You can also mix a tablespoon of borax into 2 of tablespoons of hot water, add the mixture to a gallon of warm water, and then add the sweater. Pull the sweater gently into shape, and rinse in a gallon of warm water to which you have added 2 tablespoons of vinegar.

## REDUCE CALCIUM DEPOSITS

Adding 1 to 2 tablespoons of washing soda to the detergent drawer of your washing machine will reduce calcium deposits. You'll also reduce the amount of commercial washing powder needed by 30 percent.

## KEEP WHITES BRIGHT

Add ½ a cup of baking soda to the first rinse before you wash your whites, then ¼ of a cup baking soda to the wash cycle itself. This will keep your clothes white, especially in a hard-water area.

## WANT TO KEEP YOUR JEANS FROM FADING?

Before washing them for the first time, soak your new jeans in a gallon or so of water mixed with a cup of white distilled vinegar. The colors will then fade a lot less. When washing your jeans, always remember to turn them inside out beforehand.

# HOMEMADE FABRIC CONDITIONER

Mix together 1 cup each of washing soda, distilled white vinegar, and water. Sir in a few drops of essential oil such as lavender, lemon, or geranium. Store in a screw-top bottle and use as you would commercial fabric conditioner.

# DON'T BE A STIFF

Your clothes will feel stiff after washing if you've used too much detergent. Prevent this—and save money—by cutting back on how much detergent you use, and by adding 1 cup of white vinegar to your wash load.

## RINSE CYCLE

To clean out the walls of your washing machine without commercial cleaning products, run an empty load using hot water. Also, pour 1 cup of vinegar into the machine and let it run through on this hot cycle to dissolve soap residue. Make sure not to use any detergent and that the machine is empty before doing so.

## SOAP DISPENSER

Periodically, make sure you pull out the detergent and fabric softener drawer and wash it out. You don't need chemical products to do so— just wash it in warm soapy water to clean away soap blockages, or run under the faucet. This will make your machine run more efficiently and also avoid powder build up on clothes.

## CLEAN THE OUTSIDE, TOO

Every so often wipe down the outside of your washing machine and tumble dryer. Don't use cleaning sprays, as warm, soapy water is sufficient to get rid of dirt, accumulated dust, and spilled products. Now you won't risk getting clean clothes dirty when taking them out of the machine.

## LEATHER SNEAKERS

Buff up your leather sneakers easily with this recipe.

1 tablespoon liquid castile soap

2 tablespoons distilled white vinegar

water

Mix the liquid castile soap and white vinegar into cup of warm water. Dap the mixture on a soft cloth, and buff the sneakers. Avoid machine-washing sneakers as this can damage their shape.

## LEATHER SHOES

Soften leather shoes by rubbing with lemon or castor oil rather than using commercial shoe polishes. Help prevent cracking and drying by wiping with olive oil. Treat scuffs by wiping them with the cut edge of a raw potato and then buff with a cloth afterwards.

## PRESOAK BLEND

For really tough stains, soak your clothing in this blend for 2 hours before laundering.

½ cup borax

hot water

1 cup distilled white vinegar

6 drops eucalyptus

Dissolve borax in 3 cups hot water in a bucket and allow to cool before adding other ingredients.

# HEM MARKS

To eliminate those telltale hem marks when a skirt or a pair of pants has been lengthened, dab vinegar along the marks and iron using a warm setting suitable for the material. The marks will disappear!

# BELT UP

Prolong the life of leather belts by rubbing with olive oil. Clean dirty belts and remove stains with a damp cloth or sponge dabbed in vegetable glycerin or lanolin. Wipe away the excess and buff with a dry cloth.

## SEPARATE BUT EQUAL

Always separate man-made fabrics, like polyester, from natural fibers such as cotton before filling your washing machine. Man-made fibers can attract the oils that are released from natural fibers during washing. These oils can build up, making spots more noticeable.

## LACE

If you have antique linen, lace sheets, or pillowcases, wash by hand in the bath in warm water with castile soap. Rinse with warm water, but don't wring them out. To stop the lace from pulling out of shape, pin it onto a towel that is lying flat. Store lace in tissue paper to prevent discoloration.

## WOOL CLOTHES

Instead of dry-cleaning your woolen coats, dresses, or skirts, lay them out on a table in a suitable place and sprinkle a thin, even layer of salt on top. Make a pad from a piece of folded linen and use this to rub the salt gently into the cloth with long sweeping movements (circular ones will roughen the surface). Place the garments on hangers and brush vigorously with a stiff clothes brush. Repeat on cuffs, collars, and hems as necessary.

## LOVE YOUR LEATHER, AND LET IT BREATHE

Never store your leather jacket, or any leather clothing, in plastic. That's a big mistake, because in a warm environment, water can condense inside the plastic and mildew the leather. And once leather gets mildewed, you're out of luck. There's really no way to repair it.

## PATENT LEATHER

To remove spotting from patent leather, and to make the surface shine, dab with a little milk on a clean cloth and then buff up. Alternatively, petroleum jelly smeared onto patent leather and then wiped away will also clean it and keep it in good condition.

## YOU MUST REMEMBER THIS

Always be sure to check the pockets of all garments before washing and drying. We know you know this already, but it bears repeating. The stains and damage that can result from one hidden lipstick, lip balm, stick of gum or crayon, well, we won't even consider it.

# LEATHER POLISH

If you don't want to clean your leather jacket with egg whites (see pg. 137), try using mild, soapy water, rubbing the garment, and then rinsing with a soft, clean cloth. In addition, leather can be kept in good condition by melting 2 teaspoons of grated beeswax and ¼ of a cup of olive oil in a pan. Pour into a jar and allow to cool. You can then apply a small amount of this polish every couple of months to keep it soft and supple. Rub in well and buff off any excess.

# PREVENT LIMESCALE

Take care of your steam iron by always adding distilled water, instead of tap water. It really will add to the life of your iron by preventing limescale from building up. You can also use filtered water if you keep a jug in the fridge.

## SCORCH MARKS

If you iron on too high a setting, you run the risk of scorch marks. If the affected item is 100 percent cotton, soak the scorched area in pure, freshly squeezed lemon juice. Rinse out thoroughly in warm water and leave outside to bleach naturally in the sunlight.

## STEAM CLEAN YOUR IRON

To clean the surface of an iron that is not Teflon-coated or non-stick, add 1 tablespoon of salt to ¼ cup of hot, white vinegar, and wipe this solution over the surface. To steam clean, pour equal amounts of vinegar and water into the reservoir of the iron. Turn the dial to steam and leave upright for 5 minutes. Unplug and let the iron cool down. Any loose particles will fall out when you empty the water leaving you with a clean iron.

## TOO MUCH OF A GOOD THING

Clothes should be left in the dryer just long enough to remove wrinkles and moisture. Any longer and the heat will "set" wrinkles, increase static cling, and it can cause your clothes to shrink.

## STICKY IRON?

If you've used the iron on too high a setting and something is stuck to the bottom, unplug it and allow to cool. For aluminum and chrome irons, apply a paste of baking soda and water, mixed to the consistency of toothpaste, with a soft cloth. Wipe away with a damp cloth. Treat Teflon or metallic-coated irons by rubbing a nylon scourer over the surface when cool.

## FRAGRANT IRONING

Add a wonderful fragrance to your linens by adding a couple drops of your favorite essential oil to your iron's water reservoir before ironing. Lavender is a good choice. As you iron, the room will fill with fragrance and your clothes will smell great too.

## CUT YOUR IRONING TIME IN HALF

It's easy to do. Just place a sheet of aluminum foil, shiny side up, underneath the ironing board cover. The heat generated should cut your ironing time in half.

# THE STARCH-LESS LAUNDRY ROOM

Why not make your own starch for your laundry? It's simple, cheap—and not filled with chemicals, like the commercial type. Simply combine 1 cup of cool water, 1 to 2 tablespoons of cornstarch, and a couple of drops of an essential oil (we like tea tree). Shake it up in a spray bottle, and spray on clothes as you iron!

# 10

# METALS & JEWELRY

When it's time to clean metal and jewelry in your home, resist the urge to buy expensive, toxic "made for metal" cleaners and special jewelry cleaners as well. There are plenty of natural and inexpensive ways to keep your jewelry shining clean right in this chapter— using regular non-toxic items you have in your house already.

# DRY CLEAN BRASS

Another way to clean brass is to use a dry mixture made with equal parts of salt and flour on a dry rag, adding a little vinegar if required. Rub in then buff to a shine.

## KEEP BRASS AT ITS BEST

For general upkeep, there is no need to use metal polishes. Simply wash brass pieces occasionally in warm water, with a little liquid castile soap added. Dry thoroughly. To brighten brass after polishing, rub olive oil onto it with a soft cloth.

## STAINED BRASS

To remove tarnish from brass, try sprinkling salt onto half a lemon, then rub the metal and rinse thoroughly. Bottled lemon juice mixed with salt will also be effective.

## BUTTERMILK—REALLY?

Did you know that the marks of corrosion that sometimes appear on brass will disappear if you rub them with a cloth dipped in buttermilk? It's true. After applying the buttermilk, rinse with water, and wipe dry with a soft clean cloth.

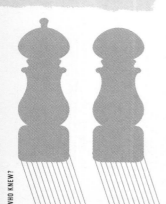

FLOUR  FLOUR

## COPPER

If the copper piece is lacquered, then it only needs dusting and the occasional wash in warm water. If the copper has become stained, however, try one of the following methods. Sprinkle salt onto half a lemon and rub the metal. Then rinse thoroughly. Bottled lemon juice mixed with salt is also effective. Buff with a soft clean cloth.

## GREAT FOR HAMBURGERS AND COPPER

Worcestershire sauce will also clean copper. Wipe it on, give it a good rub, and then rinse before polishing up with a clean soft cloth. You could also try mixing together 1 cup of vinegar, 1 cup of flour, and ½ a cup of salt. Apply this thick paste to the copper piece and leave for a few hours. Rinse thoroughly, and wipe dry with a clean cloth.

## THE IRON SOLUTION

If your iron pots and pans are a bit rusty, clean them with a vinegar-dampened cloth and some steel wool. Wipe down with the cloth, and then scrub lightly with the steel wool before rinsing and drying. Be sure to rub in a little olive oil into your pan once it is dry to prevent any further rusting.

# OXIDIZED COPPER

Spray distilled white vinegar liberally onto the surface of the copper. Then sprinkle salt over the vinegar and rub with a soft cloth. Rinse with warm water. Repeat if your copper is heavily oxidized.

# SILVER

Use a damp cloth to work white, non-gel toothpaste into the silver you want to clean, then rinse and dry. The mild abrasive in the toothpaste will clean the silver without you having to resort to chemical cleaners.

## CLEANING CAST IRON

The best way to clean cast iron pans that aren't rusty is to cover any stain with a paste of cream of tartar and white vinegar. Apply liberally, let it sit, and scrub with a damp, soft cloth.

## PEWTER

To treat any corrosion on pewter pieces, mix together 1 cup of vinegar, 1 cup of flour, and ½ a cup of salt. Apply this thick paste to the affected area and leave for a few hours. Rinse thoroughly, and wipe dry with a clean cloth.

## NEVER POLISH TARNISHED SILVERWARE AGAIN

Line your kitchen sink with aluminum foil (shiny side up), fill the sink with very hot water, and add either 1 tablespoon of salt and 1 tablespoon of baking soda or 2 tablespoons of cream of tartar. You can also simply pour in starchy water leftover from next time you cook potatoes or pasta. Immerse the silverware, leaving it to soak for up to half an hour. You'll find that the tarnish will come right off time. Remove the pieces, rinse them well, and dry with a soft cloth. Add lemon juice for really grimy silver.

## STAINED SILVER

Stains on silver can be removed by dissolving a little salt in lemon juice. Dip a soft cloth into the mixture and rub the cutlery. Rinse in warm water and finish by buffing to a shine with a chamois.

## STAINLESS STEEL

Steel wool can scratch stainless steel so never use when cleaning. Acidic or salty foods may cause pit marks. To avoid this, rinse stainless steel soon after use and wash in hot soapy water. Any baked-on food can be removed with a paste of baking soda and water.

## ANOTHER REASON TO LOVE BAKING SODA

Baking soda is safe and effective when it comes to cleaning gold and silver jewelry. For best results, use a paste of baking soda and hydrogen peroxide, and rub gently on your jewelry. It gets rid of dirt, grime and body oils, and leaves your gold and silver sparkling.

# STORE SILVER WITH CHALK

To prevent silver cutlery from tarnishing, place a few pieces of chalk in the drawer with it, as this will absorb any moisture. Store the chalk and silver in air-tight plastic bags, and tarnish will be a thing of the past.

# WATER MARKS ON STAINLESS STEEL

Remove hard-water spots from stainless steel by polishing with a clean dry cloth. Stubborn spots can be removed with a cloth soaked in undiluted white vinegar. Avoid abrasive cleaners, as they will dull the finish of your stainless steel.

## TIN, A FEATHER DUSTER, A POTATO AND YOU

If you've got any elaborately decorated tin, use a feather duster to clean, or wipe with a dry or slightly damp cloth. Wash in a mild solution of natural dishwashing liquid and warm water with a soft cloth. Avoid abrasive scrubbing brushes and cleaners as these may scratch through the plating and cause rust. And speaking of rust, if you rub half a potato over the rust spot, it will disappear.

## IT'S EASY TO CLEAN CHROME

Mix distilled white vinegar and salt, and apply to chrome using a soft cloth. Rinse well with water and buff to brilliance with a dry cloth. Half a lemon lightly dipped in salt will work just as well, and chrome will shine beautifully if you give it a rub with a piece of aluminum foil. Try white flour to help you get the finger marks off chrome.

## AMBER

Wipe amber jewelry with a soft cloth wrung out in warm soapy water. Dry at once because water makes amber cloudy. Wipe with sweet almond oil to remove any grease marks.

## GOLD AND PLATINUM

Occasionally wipe gold and platinum with a soft, clean chamois. Ordinary cloths can hold onto grit that can damage the metal's surface. Gold plate should be treated with care as the thin layer may rub off with excessive polishing.

## KEEP AWAY

Never store diamonds with other gemstones, particularly pearls. Diamonds can easily scratch your other pieces of jewelry.

# JEWELRY

Most precious stones, with the exception of pearls, can be cleaned in warm soapy water with a soft toothbrush. Rinse in clean water and dry thoroughly.

### Who Knew?

Gold and copper were the first discovered around 5000BC.

# PRECIOUS AND SEMI-PRECIOUS STONES

Gentle soap and water plus a soft cloth are all that is need to clean citrines, turquoise, and garnets. Don't be fooled into buying expensive jewelry cleaners.

## THE SIMPLEST DIAMOND, AMETHYST, RUBY AND SAPPHIRE CLEANER EVER

Diamonds can be cleaned in a bit of undiluted dish-washing liquid. Scrub gently with a soft toothbrush. Rinse in lukewarm water to remove any detergent film. Drain on a towel and buff with a chamois. Amethysts, rubies, and sapphires can also be cleaned in this way.

## WEAR YOUR PEARLS

The best way to care for a pearl (or coral) necklace is to wear it regularly because oils in your skin add a gentle luster. After wearing, wipe with a chamois to remove traces of perspiration that can damage the surface. Wash in water and very mild soap, then wipe with a soft cloth. Lay on moist paper towels to dry. Pearls can also be rubbed with a few drops of vegetable glycerin and buffed to a shine.

## Who Knew?

Over 100 tons of earth are mined get one diamond large enough to cut into a one-carat stone.

## MARCASITE

It's simple to bring back a shine to marcasite by polishing with a soft brush and then buff with a chamois. Marcasite should never be washed.

## TURQUOISE AND OPALS

Turquoise and opals are porous stones, so never immerse them in water. Instead polish with a soft, dry chamois and clean claws with a soft bristle brush.

## EMERALDS

Emeralds are softer than other precious stones and therefore can chip easily. Wash carefully in a warm solution of water and dishwashing liquid.

# TANGLED NECKLACES

For annoying tangles in thin necklaces or bracelets, place on a glass surface. Add a drop of baby oil and use a pin to tease out the knots. Rinse in warm water.

## Who Knew?

A single ounce of gold can be drawn into a wire 60 miles long.

# 11

# HEALTH &
# BEAUTY

In this chapter, you'll find plenty of natural tips and simple recipes to keep feeling and looking your best, without spending a fortune.

# TEA TREE

Tea tree oil is a great alternative to chemical healing ointments and balms. A natural antiseptic, it's terrific in emergencies for cuts and grazes as well as for cleaning up after animals (or children) who have not been housetrained.

## ARNICA FOR WOUNDS

Help your wounds heal with arnica instead of highly packaged and produced creams designed to do the same job. Arnica is a perennial plant that is available in cream form to help soothe muscle aches, reduces inflammation, reduce bruising, and it's great for skin problems such as acne and insect bites. Do not use on broken skin or of you suffer from skin sensitivity.

## ALOE FOR STINGS

Don't invest in chemical creams for stings and bruises when natural products will do just as well to help you heal quickly. Aloe vera is a great soothing product that can be used on itchy skin. It also helps bites and stings to heal and can ease the pain of burns. Aloe vera produces around six different antiseptics, which can kill mold, bacteria, and fungus. It also is a wonderful cleanser for your skin.

## FRESH BREATH

Ditch your chemical mouthwash and try squeezing a lemon into a glass of warm water. Hold the liquid in your mouth for 60 seconds before spitting out.

## BANISH BODY ODOR

You can mix equal parts of organic apple cider vinegar and water, and pat this onto your armpits and any other nasty area where perspiration is a problem. Wait for it to dry before applying a natural deodorant.

## HYDROGEN PEROXIDE IS YOUR FRIEND

If your underarms are feeling, well, not so fresh, reach for the peroxide. Just put two teaspoons in a cup of water and wash out your pits. It really works.

# HEADACHES

Instead of popping pills at the first sign of a headache, try a one-minute trick to relieve tension. Press the tips of your fingers together, apply pressure, and breathe slowly, and count to 60 while concentrating on your breathing.

# NAILS

Instead of taking chemical supplements for good nail growth, try adding wild seaweed to your diet as it contains more vitamins and minerals than nearly any other food.

## GOOD DIGESTION

You can boost your digestive system by eating a little spicy, pickled food before your main meal. Try eating ginger or pickled cabbage. This will save on indigestion pills later.

## PERSONAL INSECT REPELLENT

Make a sweet smelling insect repellent easily, and stop spraying yourself with store bought pesticides.

    1 ½ teaspoon citronella essential oil

    1 ½ teaspoon lavender essential oil

    ¾ teaspoon eucalyptus essential oil

    1 teaspoon jojoba essential oil

    8 fl. oz. distilled witch hazel

Mix the oils together in glass spray bottle. Shake well and then add the distilled witch hazel. Shake again and spray on your body and clothes when needed, avoiding the eyes.

## TENSION HEADACHE

Try this relaxing herbal tea for relieving tension headaches without painkillers.

>    1 teaspoon fresh ginger

>    water

>    1 teaspoon dried chamomile

>    1 teaspoon dried linden

>    honey

Simmer the fresh ginger in 1 cup of water in a covered pan for 5 minutes. Remove the pan from the heat and add the chamomile and linden. Leave for 10 minutes, then strain, and sweeten with honey if needed, before drinking the hot tea.

## HERBAL TEA

Another herbal tea to try for headaches and stress is made with chamomile and catnip. Pour boiling water over 1 teaspoon each of dried chamomile and catnip. Cover and leave for 10 minutes. Strain and sweeten if needed.

# SINUS HEADACHE

Spicy foods may relieve the congestion causing sinus headaches without the need for painkillers, by increasing the flow of blood and loosening the mucus in your sinuses.

# WALK IT OFF

One of the simplest solutions for stress is to take a brisk walk. Exercise will stimulate endorphins in your body, which will lift your mood without taking any pills. Try walking for 30 to 45 minutes.

## PASSION FLOWER TEA

Try this tea before bedtime for a restful night's sleep. Pour 1 cup of boiling water over 1 teaspoon each of dried passion flower and chamomile. Cover and leave for 10 minutes before straining and drinking.

## HOT AND COLD HEADACHE TREATMENT

To relieve a headache try putting an ice cold compress over the area where pain is felt. Make a footbath with the hottest water you can put your feet in comfortably. This should increase the flow of blood to the feet, thereby reducing blood flow in the head and reducing headache pain.

## ST JOHN'S WORT

This is a natural antidepressant and it is widely available. Try taking 300mg, three times a day. Do be aware that St John's Wort can interfere with other medicines including contraceptives so do check with a doctor or pharmacist before taking.

## SLEEP WELL

Tips to help you get a good night's sleep include relaxing before sleeping by reading a book or listening to calming music, or taking a warm bath. Make sure your bedroom is free from electronic equipment and distractions and ensure it is well ventilated and not too warm and keep to the same bedtime routine. Try all these things before resorting to chemical sleeping pills.

# EARACHE

Try a heat pad or hot water bottle in a cover placed over the ear to reduce the pain from earache before taking painkillers. Also, half an onion wrapped in a damp, warm face cloth and applied to the ear is known to be effective as well.

# MELATONIN

Melatonin is a hormone produced by your body that tells
you when it is time to sleep.
You can take these natural
supplements to aid sleep in
your new time zone but make
sure you follow instructions
about when to take it to get
the best results, depending
on whether you are flying
east or west.

## MINIMIZE JET LAG

Flying during the day if possible is one natural way
to minimize jet lag. Getting into a routine when you
get to your destination will help you adjust. Try not
to nap when you arrive and don't take sleeping pills;
instead try to settle into the timings of the time zone
you are in. Sunshine is also a great natural tonic for
getting rid of jetlag in place of any commercial jet
lag remedies. If you are suffering, make sure you go
out into the sunlight as soon as possible because this
will help to reset your body clock.

## EXERCISE

Exercise is also a great, free way to overcome jet lag.
Try a brisk walk, as this should help you relax and
also help you get to sleep without pills. Keep up
regular exercise when on vacation because this will
strengthen the body's resilience.

## GETTING RID OF CANKER SORES

Rinse your mouth twice a day with a mix of ½ a teaspoon of sea salt dissolved in ½ a cup of warm water. Also, try avoiding highly acidic foods such as tomatoes, citrus fruit, pineapple, and vinegar.

## HOW ABOUT BANISHING CANKER SORES FOREVER?

Hydrogen peroxide is not just a terrific bleach substitute—if you just take one capful a day, and swish it around for a full 10 minutes in your mouth, it's effective at preventing canker sores. Mix a capful with water and give it a try. It also has been shown to whiten teeth, too.

## LICORICE FOR CANKER SORES

Another more long-term treatment for canker sores is to try DGL (deglycyrrhizinated licorice) as you can take this for up to three months. DGL will stimulate your body to produce mucus and encourage healing. Look for chewable DGL tablets at your health food store and follow the directions on the bottle.

# ECHINACEA

Echinacea is believed to boost the immune system so take these natural supplements if you need a boost or feel a cold coming on try it. Children over six can take half a teaspoon of Echinacea extract three times a day.

# CHARCOAL FOR STINGS

Charcoal paste can be made and used to draw out toxins from bites and stings. You can also buy activated charcoal capsules, which you can open and use with a few drops of water on the sting or bite. Leave for 30 minutes then wash off paste.

## FOOT SOAK

Try a calendula foot soak to ward off athlete's foot and promote skin healing. Pour 2 cups of boiling water over 4 tablespoons of dried calendula flowers. Leave until it cools to lukewarm, add ¼ of a cup of apple cider vinegar, then pour into a footbath and soak feet.

## FOOT SPRAY

This foot spray soothes itching and combats fungus. Mix 4 fl oz of aloe vera juice with ½ a teaspoon of tea tree oil in a spray bottle. Shake well and spray onto feet. Allow to dry fully. To be sure of the fungus not returning, use for a few weeks after the itching has stopped.

## FOR STINKY FEET

Apple cider vinegar is really effective at controlling foot odor. Just soak your feet several times a week in a cup or two of vinegar added to a small pan of warm water for the best results.

## TEA TREE FOR WARTS

Tea tree oil can eliminate warts due to its powerful antiviral nature. Dab neat tea tree oil with a cotton bud directly onto the wart several times a day until it has gone.

## GARLIC FOR WARTS

Garlic also has strong antiviral properties and can be used as a poultice. First protect the skin around the wart by smearing with vitamin E oil from a capsule. Mash a clove of garlic and put this paste over the wart. Cover with a bandage and leave for 24 hours. A blister should form and the wart will hopefully fall off within a week.

## DANDELION FOR WARTS?

An old time remedy for warts is to break open the stem of a dandelion and rub the milky sap on the warts in a circular motion. Do this two or three times a day, and in a week or so, the wart should be gone.

# COLD SORES

If you are prone to cold sores, which are caused by the herpes virus, try rubbing an ice cube on the affected area at the first sign of the telltale tingle. If done early, this can be an effective treatment for inhibiting cold sores from fully developing.

### Who Knew?

Another old wives' tale bites the dust: sitting close to a television screen in no way damages your eyes.

# WITCH HAZEL FOR BLISTERS

To heal a blister, try applying a cotton ball soaked in witch hazel extract to the blister and covering with a bandage. Change the cotton regularly.

## BURNS

To speed up the healing of burns and fight infection use this aloe vera solution.

- ½ cup peeled, sliced aloe leaf
- 1,000mg powdered vitamin C
- 800 IU vitamin E oil
- 1 teaspoon of lavender oil

In a sterilized blender, mix all ingredients. Put the mixture in a sterilized glass jar and keep refrigerated for up to 2 months. Apply it several times a day to the burn. (You can sterilize equipment in a hot dishwasher or in a warm oven.)

## ALOE FOR BLISTERS

You can also speed up healing of blisters by covering them with a thin slice of peeled aloe vera. Again cover with a bandage and change twice a day until healed.

## SINUS CONGESTION

Eucalyptus and peppermint oils will help open the nasal passages and loosen the mucus. Pour boiling water into a sink or large bowl and then add 5 drops of eucalyptus oil and 2 drops of peppermint oil. Put a towel over your head and inhale the steam from the water, taking care because the water will be very hot.

## COUGH MEDICINE

For a natural cough mixture, add a squeeze of lemon juice to ½ a teaspoon of honey. Let this dissolve in your mouth before swallowing and repeat as needed throughout the day. Not suitable for children under 2 years old.

## CURING A COUGH NATURALLY

If you're sick with a cold and bad cough, try and drink at least 8 eight-ounce glasses of water a day. Water is the best expectorant there is, and it will help loosen the cough. Eating hot chilli peppers also helps to loosen mucus.

# EASE A COUGH AT NIGHT

To ease coughing and blocked passages at night, try dabbing some peppermint oil under your nose, or, if you have sensitive skin, use 1 or 2 drops on your pillow. The strong scent should break up congestion and help you sleep better.

# SORE THROAT SOLUTION

To relieve a sore throat, gargle several times a day with ½ a cup of warm water, mixed with 1 tablespoon of lemon juice, 1 tablespoon of salt, and a dash of cayenne. Alternatively, try hot fresh lemon juice together with 1 teaspoon of honey.

## SAGE FOR A SORE THROAT

Another gargling solution for sore throats can be made by pouring 1 cup of boiling water over 2 teaspoons of dried sage. Cover and leave for 10 minutes then strain, add ½ a teaspoon of sea salt, and stir.

## NATURAL SORE THROAT REMEDY

Here's our favorite sore throat remedy of all: Fill a shot glass with honey, and warm in the microwave for about 10 seconds. Add ¼ teaspoon cinnamon, stir, and drink. Repeat a few times a day. In three days, you'll feel much better!

## TEA FOR INDIGESTION

This herbal tea helps relieve indigestion and eases pain, along with stimulating digestive juices. Simmer 1 teaspoon of fresh chopped ginger root and ½ a teaspoon of fennel seeds in 1 cup of water for 5 minutes. Remove from the heat and add ½ a teaspoon of dried peppermint. Cover and leave for 10 minutes. Strain and sweeten with honey if needed.

## MASSAGE AWAY CONGESTION

Use the following natural massage oil to relieve the congestion and aches and pains associated with a cold: Mix 4 fl oz of almond oil with 20 drops each of eucalyptus and lavender oils and 5 drops of peppermint oil.

## EXOTIC MASSAGE OIL

Mix 2 fl oz of almond oil with 16 drops of ylang ylang, 12 drops of geranium oil, 10 drops of sandalwood oil, 8 drops of patchouli oil, and 6 drops of clary sage oil and shake to combine. Massage into the skin to improve circulation.

## AN OLD-FASHIONED REMEDY FOR CALLUSES

If you're troubled by hard calluses on your feet, try this old-fashioned but effective remedy: Grind a few aspirins into a paste with equal parts lemon juice and water. Apply it to the calluses, then rap your feet in a hot towel, cover in a plastic bag, and stay off your feet for ½ hour. When you unrap your feet, the calluses should be ready to filed off with a pumice stone.

# CAYENNE FOR PAIN RELIEF

Cayenne has anti-inflammatory, antiseptic, diuretic, and analgesic properties. To ease gas and stomach cramps or to help promote digestion, a tea can be made by adding ¼ of a teaspoon of cayenne to 1 cup of hot water. Chewing on a hot pepper may provide temporary relief from toothache. You can also buy cayenne cream or ointment for arthritis.

# FUNGAL NAIL INFECTION

Tea tree oil is a great anti-bacterial, so try a few drops directly onto the infected nail a few times each day. Also, try soaking your feet daily in a mix of half apple cider vinegar and half water.

## HONEY FIGHTS INFECTION

Unprocessed honey contains a natural antibiotic that guards against infection. To use it, clean the wound, smooth on a thin layer of honey, and cover with a bandage. Reapply and change the dressing twice a day.

## SUNBURN AND WINDBURN

Cover the burnt skin with light clothing or a towel, and get into the shade! Sponge the affected area with cold water and stay hydrated. Do not break any blisters. Apply calamine lotion to mild burns rather than a commercial burn cream, but if burns are severe, seek medical help as soon as possible.

## TOO MUCH SUN?

Alleviate sunburn pain by making tea, cooling it, and applying it  to the burn. All teas will help, but peppermint or spearmint are especially good. Teas have tannins that help the heal burns. For a severe sunburn, fill the bathtub with tea and take a nice, long soak.

## STINGS AND ITCHING

Light rashes such as mosquito bites and poison ivy may be treated naturally with calamine lotion. Washing and cleaning products can irritate your skin so if in doubt, change them. If problems persist, consult your doctor.

## WASP AND BEE STINGS II

Believe it or not, meat tenderizer works wonders on all sorts of stings—bee, wasps, even jellyfish. Make a paste with tenderizer and water, and rub on the bite. Tenderizer has papain, which helps break down the proteins n insect venom.

## WASP AND BEE STINGS III

Rub undiluted lavender essential oil directly onto the sting or mix up a paste of 1 teaspoon baking soda and a little water or vinegar. Apply directly to the sting.

# WASP AND BEE STINGS

Slice an onion in half and rub the cut side over a bee or wasp sting to ease the pain instead of using chemical sprays.

# MORNING OR TRAVEL SICKNESS

Ginger will soothe the digestive system and is safe to take during pregnancy. Drink ginger tea made by adding fresh ginger slices to hot water or alternatively chew a little piece of the root.

## CATNIP INSECT REPELLENT

For an effective insect repellent, rub fresh catnip leaves over the exposed skin or use extract of catnip.

## COLD CURE

Don't reach for the painkillers for a cold. Finely chop a few garlic cloves, cover with honey and leave for 2 to 3 hours. Take teaspoons throughout the day. Also, keep hydrated by drinking plenty of fluids.

## HANGOVER

The best way to stop a hangover is to eat two apples as soon as you wake up. This will replace lost vitamins and reduce the effects of dehydration, as will eating a banana, which is a great source of potassium and magnesium, both of which need replacing after drinking too much alcohol.

## A NATURAL TOOTHACHE TREATMENT

Place 1 to 2 drops of clove essential oil on a cotton ball and dab onto the sore area. If you cannot stand the bitter taste, try rubbing fresh figs into gums as these have anti-inflammatory properties. Of course, consult your dentist as well.

## TENSION HEADACHE TREATMENT

Message a few drops of eucalyptus oil into your forehead and sniff the oil as you do so. Eucalyptus is known to help relieve tension headaches.

## HAVE YOU GOT THE FEVER?

An old-fashioned remedy for mild fever is to mix 1½ teaspoons cream of tartar with ½ teaspoon lemon juice in a pint of water, flavored with honey. Drink a glass a few times a day, and watch it help your fever.

## NATURAL PAINKILLER

Unseed 3 small chilies, and blend with 1 pint of tomato juice and a dash of soy sauce. Drink as much as you can to release endorphins into the body.

# UPSET STOMACH

Try a cup of black tea or drink a little fresh lemon or lime juice mixed with water to ease a stomach ache instead of reaching for painkillers.

## GINGER FOR HEADACHES

To ease tension from headaches, mix 2 tablespoons ground ginger with a little water and warm gently in a saucepan. Spread the mixture onto a washcloth, and lie down in a dark and quiet room with the cloth pressed on your forehead.

## SMALL CUTS AND WOUNDS

Apply undiluted lavender essential oil to burns or cuts to help them heal quickly. This also helps prevent scarring. Keep small cuts clean and germ-free with the cut side of a piece of garlic or onion.

## INDIGESTION AND HEARTBURN

Try treating indigestion or heartburn by drinking 1 teaspoon of baking soda mixed with 1fl oz of water before reaching for remedies made with chemicals. It really works wonderfully.

## HAIR CONDITIONER

Don't waste money on expensive hair conditioning treatments when you can make your own. Just mash an avocado and mix with either aloe vera or mayonnaise to make a paste. Spread onto hair and comb with a wide tooth comb. Wrap up hair and leave for 30 minutes before washing off and rinsing. A mixture of mashed banana with olive oil works well, too.

## HAIR MASK

You can use olive oil as a moisturizing hair mask without having to rely on chemical products with lots of packaging. Simply smooth it on to hair and then wash out.

## A CORNY TIP

To get rid of bothersome corns naturally, soak a small cloth in apple cider vinegar and bind it on the corn, and leave it on for a day or two. The corn should disappear. You can also try and soak your feet in a shallow pan of warm water with half a cup of the vinegar. With either treatment, finish by rubbing the corn with a clean pumice stone.

# OLIVE OIL

Don't forget, olive oil isn't just a staple for your kitchen cupboard—it's also a great choice for moisturizing your skin in place of commercial lotions and potions.

# GREEN TEA RINSE

Go green in more ways than one by washing your hair in cooled green tea, thought to have natural antibacterial properties that will help reduce scalp sensitivity and will cut down dandruff. But don't worry, it won't turn your hair green!

## NATURAL OILS

Instead of using a moisturizer filled with the latest chemical products, use natural oils. Almond oil is a great favorite for sensitive areas, or use hemp or flax oil for hands.

## VEGGIE ROOTS

Next time you get your roots touched up at the hair salon, ask for vegetable-based dye rather than chemical alternatives. Not only is it better for the environment, it's also better for your health as you won't absorb potential toxins.

## LARYNGITIS TREATMENT

To regain your voice, try this remedy: Peel a piece of ginger root, and cut 5 slices into a small pot of boiling water to make a tea. Add honey, and sip the tea slowly, while clearing your throat. The ginger will tingle a bit, and your voice should be restored.

## MAKE YOUR OWN PERFUME

Experiment making your own perfume so you can stop spraying yourself with chemicals. Take 1 cup of fresh chopped flower blossoms and place into a bowl lined with cheesecloth. Pour 2 cups of water over the flowers until they are covered. Cover and leave overnight. The next day, using the edges of the cheesecloth, pull it out of the bowl and gently squeeze the scented water into a small pot. Simmer the water until about 1 tablespoon is left. Cool and place into a small bottle. This perfume keeps for one month; store it in the refrigerator for best results.

## MAKE AFTERSHAVE

Try this aftershave and you'll never buy another.

> 3 drops lemongrass essential oil
>
> 10 drops lavender essential oil
>
> 10 drops lime essential oil
>
> 1 cup vodka
>
> distilled water

Combine the oils and pour into a glass bottle. Shake well. Leave for 3 weeks. Add 1 cup of distilled water then leave for another week. Shake once a day. Store in dark bottles and keep in a cool dark place.

# SAY NO TO SCENTS

The majority of fragrances are made entirely from petrochemical products, which are very damaging to the environment. They can contain phthalates that have been shown to damage the lungs, liver, and kidneys. Instead of buying petrochemical perfume, make your own with a few drops of essential oil in rosewater or carrier oil.

# PRE-MAKE UP

Rosewater makes an excellent natural spritzer to spray onto the oily parts of your face before applying your make up.

## MAKE UP REMOVAL

Instead of using disposable tissues, wipes, or lotions to take off your make up, why not keep a thin piece of cheesecloth in your bathroom for this and use with water only? It is washable and dries quickly.

## FACE MASK

Mix 2 tablespoons of rosewater with 1 tablespoon of natural yogurt and 1 tablespoon of manuka honey. Apply the mask to your T-zone (nose and forehead) and leave for 10 minutes before rinsing it off.

## DRY LIPS?

Mix manuka honey with a little olive oil and smooth onto lips to relieve dryness and soreness the natural way without resorting to chemical lip balms.

## IT'S WHITE VINEGAR FOR NOSEBLEEDS

Distilled white vinegar is effective in stopping nosebleeds. Just dampen a cotton ball and plug the nostril. The acetic acid in the vinegar cauterizes the wound.

## FOR THE SOFTEST HANDS, NATURALLY

For a natural hand mask, mix mashed potatoes with milk (either cow's milk or soy). Work into a creamy paste, apply to your hands, and leave for 2 to 3 minutes before rinsing off. Your hands will feel wonderfully soft and smooth.

## GREEN HAIR?

If you are a regular in the pool, your hair is probably not in the best condition. Try a touch of tomato ketchup on your hair before you wash it, as this will counteract any green tinge, which develops from the pool chemicals reacting with your hair, especially if your hair is colored. Smooth the ketchup onto your hair and leave for 10 minutes before washing out.

## THE NATURAL EXFOLIATER

Rubbing a slice of pineapple or papaya onto your skin will help remove dead skin cells. Leave for 5 minutes then rinse off with water. Alternatively, use olive oil mixed with salt for an abrasive action.

# TIRED EYES?

Rather than buying an eye pack, soak a cloth in rose-water or cold milk and press the pads onto tired eyes. Relax for 10 minutes and you will feel invigorated. Sliced cucumbers are also nice on tired, puffy eyes.

# 12

# BABIES & PETS

# DO YOU REALLY WANT TO DOUSE YOUR KIDS IN PESTICIDES?

If you've got kids, chances are you're familiar with lice. The next time those little bugs infest your kids, don't reach for the pesticide-laden shampoo that's commonly used. Simply soak your child's head in olive oil, and wash with dishwashing liquid. The entire treatment can be found at www.essortment. com. Just type in "natural lice treatment" as keywords once you get to the site.

## TEA TREE FOR HEAD LICE

If you don't want to go the olive oil route, forget about the chemical shampoos, as head lice are becoming resistant to.  But you can try tea tree, instead. Make a conditioning rinse with your usual conditioner, a splash of white vinegar, and a few drops of tea tree oil, then comb through thoroughly once a week until the lice are gone.

## COLIC RELIEF

Cow's milk can cause colic in bottle-fed infants. But breast-fed babies can also be affected so nursing mothers should avoid cow's milk, caffeine, and spicy food. Other foods to be avoided include eggs, garlic, citrus fruits, and cabbage. For colic relief, pour 1 cup of boiling water over 1 teaspoon each of dried chamomile and fennel seeds. Strain and cool, and give your baby a small amount via a dropper as needed.

## BABY WIPES

If you want to use baby wipes but are concerned about waste, why not make your own wipes? Just use cotton squares dipped in water, and then mixed with vinegar, aloe vera, and lavender or tea tree oil. Keep in a sealed container and launder when used.

## WHITEN DIAPERS

Instead of using chemical disinfectant or bleach on diapers, pre-soak in 3 tablespoons of baking soda dissolved in warm water in either a tub or washing machine for whiter-than-white results. Where possible, always dry diapers in the fresh air and sunshine.

# FOR THE CLEANEST DIAPERS

Keep your baby clean and happy with this recipe.

- ½ cup borax
- ¼ cup distilled white vinegar
- tea tree oil

Simply mix the borax, vinegar, and 6 drops of tea tree oil in a bucket of hot water. Soak the diapers for 45 minutes, and if possible, lie them out in the sun to dry, They'll be clean as can be until you put them back on your baby. And remember, not only are cloth diapers much environmentally friendly than the disposable variety, they're cheaper, too!

# BABY OIL

Petroleum-based baby oils and creams are harsh to manufacture and can block the skin's natural ability to breathe. Use natural oils such as almond and olive oil instead.

## DIAPER PAIL

Plastics tend to absorb odors so if you're diaper pail is plastic, you're in trouble. When it needs cleaning, try adding 1 teaspoon of tea tree oil to 1 cup of distilled white vinegar, and soaking it in the scented vinegar for a few hours before rinsing.

## SUPER-CLEAN STROLLERS

Clean strollers with a sprinkling of baking soda on a damp cloth. Wipe down and rinse with warm water. More persistent marks can be removed with the suds (not water) from a solution of water and dishwashing liquid.

## WE HATE DIAPER RASHES

An effective and natural way to soothe diaper rash is by adding a cup of baking soda to your baby's bathwater.

## CAT LITTER BOXES

Add 12 drops of eucalyptus or peppermint oil to 1 cup of baking soda and mix well. Pour the scented mixture into the bottom of the litter box then add cat litter or sand. You'll get a lovely clean smell as the oils permeate the plastic, and it will be easier to clean, too.

## DID MITTENS COUGH UP A FUR BALL?

To remove fresh vomit from a hard surface, pour cat litter over it so it can be absorbed. Sweep up and wipe the surface with a damp sponge. Lift solids from carpets and sponge with cool water. Sprinkle with baking soda and dry. Vacuum and sponge with a solution of dishwashing liquid and water. Rinse and blot dry.

## FLEA FREE

Fleas can be eliminated from furniture and carpet by vacuuming with a high-powered cleaner, (ideally with a canister) with a bag that seals tightly. Remove the bag as soon as you're done, and throw it away.

# COMB AWAY FLEAS

Don't sprinkle pesticide onto your pet's fur or use a flea collar. Instead, bathe it regularly using tea tree oil added to the water, then comb out any pests.

# PETS OUTSIDE

Pet urine on your lawn can make the grass turn brown in patches. If you catch your dog or cat urinating on your lawn, soak the area with water as soon as possible to reduce the potency of the urine on your grass.

## CARPET STAINS

If you pet's accidents leave any stains on the carpet, try the following as soon as possible.

> ¼ cup distilled white vinegar
>
> 1 teaspoon natural dishwashing soap
>
> water

Mix the distilled white vinegar into ¼ of a cup of water, and natural dishwashing soap.  Pour into a spray bottle and shake well. Blot the stain with paper towels then spray on the cleaner. Blot again and rinse.

## PET FECES

If your pet has an accident, scrape away any solids, then sponge well with a solution of ¼ of a cup of vinegar and 2 cups of water. Sprinkle the area with baking soda, leave for a few hours, and vacuum clean.

## THE BEST NATURAL DISINFECTANT

For an alternative disinfectant that really works when you absolutely need it (for instance, when toilet training young animals) and also gets rid of grease and even attacks rust, mix 3 to 6 tablespoons of eucalyptus oil with 2 pints of water and decant into a spray bottle. Shake before use and keep in the fridge for up to a month.

## SALT AWAY FLEAS

If you've got a doghouse in your garden that you want to keep flea-free without using harmful chemicals, simply give the floor a sprinkling of salt to keep the pests at bay and your pet happy and healthy.

## IS FIDO FREAKING? IS PUPPY IN A PANIC?

Believe it or not, oats are wonderful for calming nervous dogs and boosting their nervous system. A daily or weekly helping of cooked oatmeal added to your pet's food also provides a good source of fiber.

# PREVENT FLEAS

Instead of resorting to chemical treatments, every day add one garlic capsule to your pet's food. This helps prevent roundworm and also deters fleas.

# PET BEDDING

Be sure to vacuum and mop regularly around and beneath pet beds as well as their favorite places around the home. Blot up urine as soon as you spot it. Rinse area in vinegar and water solution, blot, and dry.

## IS YOUR POOCH NOT SO FRESH?

If your pet is making the house smell, sprinkle baking soda all over the offending carpet or rug. Leave for at least 15 minutes and then vacuum.

## CORNMEAL FOR CARPETS

Cornmeal is another good carpet deodorizer to use if you have pets. Try mixing 8 fl oz of cornmeal with 4 fl oz of borax. Sprinkle on the carpet and leave for 15 minutes before vacuuming it up.

## HEALTHY PETS, NATURALLY

Vitamins and minerals are important to your pet's health. Save the water from steamed or boiled vegetables, and mix it with your pet's food for extra nutrients.

## QUICK HAIR PICK-UP

Instead of getting out the vacuum cleaner, try this miraculous trick to remove animal hair from fabric or carpets. Drag a damp sponge in small bursts over the surface. The hairs will stick to the moist sponge and leave the area hair-free. Rinse the sponge frequently. Another method is to put on a pair of dishwashing gloves and drag your hands along the animal hair, which will adhere to the gloves.

## FLEAS

If your pets are infested with ticks or fleas, prepare an herbal rinse by placing some rosemary in boiling water and allowing it to cool. Wash the pet well with soap and warm water, dry thoroughly, and then apply the rinse. Do not towel down your pet, as this will remove the residue, but make sure your pet is dry before letting him or her out.

## HELP FOR TEETHING PUPPIES

Help your teething friend out by making chicken or beef broth ice cubes. Puppies love the taste and chewing the ice, as it soothes their teeth, and makes them feel better. It beats chewing on your shoes, right?

### Who Knew?

Fur balls be gone! If your cat is troubled by hairballs, just apply a drop of petroleum jelly to his nose. When he licks it off, it will prevent future hairballs from developing.

# 13

# PESTS

# KEEP WEEVILS AT BAY

Take non-perishable items such as beans and grains out of plastic bags and put into sealed glass containers and keep in a cool, dark place. You can also place a couple of bay leaves in the containers, as this will repel weevils.

## DETER MOTHS

Camphor bricks or lavender bags will keep moths at bay. In addition, they leave everything in your closet smelling delicious. In time their smell fades, so change them once a year. Essential oils such as cedar, eucalyptus, and lavender dabbed on handkerchief or pieces of cotton and stored with your clothes will also do the same job.

## ANTS

To get rid of ants without resorting to chemicals, locate the entrance to the nest, squeeze a lemon onto it and leave the peel there too. Ants will also retreat from lines of talcum powder, chalk, bone meal, charcoal dust, and cayenne pepper. For some reason ants also dislike cinnamon so place it wherever you have noticed them.

## BASIL, BAY LEAVES, AND BUGS

A great way to eliminate crawling bugs in your kitchen drawers is to crumble a few bay leaves along with basil leaves. Bugs hate them. You should also crumble a few leaves for your windowsill as well.

## MOTHS

To trap moths, mix 1 part sugar syrup with 2 parts white vinegar and place it in a margarine or yogurt container. Clean it out regularly. Cedar chips and black pepper also both work well as all-natural moth deterrents. Simply put either one in a cloth bag, and when placed in drawers or hung up, they will deter moths.

## RODENTS

If you leave rodent poison in your kitchen or roof space, you can't control the amount of poison they ingest. You will also run the risk of harm to domestic pets or family members who may encounter the poison. Traps are a much greener way to get rid of them. If you're squeamish, place a brown paper lunch bag around a baited mousetrap. The mice seem drawn to exploring a small space and all you have to do is close the bag and dispose of it once they've been caught.

# MOTHPROOF YOUR CLOTHES

Mothproof your clothes using a mixture of lavender oil and cedarwood oil, which are natural moth repellents. Simply add a few drops of each oil to a spray bottle filled with water, and spray your closet. Commercial moth repellents usually contain para-dichlorobenzene (p-DCB), a carcinogenic toxic. Very high usage of p-DCB products in the home can result in dizziness, headaches, and liver problems.

# KEEP SPIDERS HAPPY

Don't kill spiders—they are important pest killers. Try and co-exist with them in your house and in your garden, remembering that they're doing you a favor by keeping your space pest free without the need for chemicals.

## SILVERFISH

To trap silverfish, mix up 1 part each of corn syrup and molasses to 2 parts white vinegar. Place the mixture near cracks and holes where pests live. Silverfish can also be repelled by treating table legs and cracks in cupboards with a mixture of borax and honey.

## FIERY PLANT SPRAY

Instead of using pesticides for houseplants, blend 2 or 3 very hot chili peppers, half an onion, and a clove of garlic in water, boil, and then allow to cool and transfer to a sealed container. Leave for two days and strain. Used as a spray, this liquid is good for indoor and outdoor plants and can be frozen for future use.

## SHINE ON

Deer and other large animals are afraid of anything shiny. If you want to keep your property deer free, hang strips of aluminum foil from trees or shrubbery.

## ESSENTIAL OIL FOR ANTS

Planting herbs such as lavender or peppermint in the ground or in pots will deter ants. You could also try placing small pots of mint on your windowsill. Alternatively, put a few drops of either peppermint or citronella oil onto cloth and place where you have ants. Refresh the oil every other day.

## TRAP ANTS

In a screw top jar, mix the following: 3 cups of water, 1 cup of sugar, and 4 teaspoons of boric acid. Poke holes in the lid and put the jar outside near the ants but out of the reach of pets and children.

## MOSQUITO SOLUTION

Eliminate the itch of mosquito bites by applying rubbing alcohol and soap. It will make the bites virtually disappear.

# ANT POWDER

To make your own natural ant powder, mix together ¼ of a cup of each of the following: dried peppermint leaves, cayenne powder, and borax. Sprinkle the mixture around the area where the ants are coming into your home.

# FLY PAPER

Instead of buying chemical fly paper from shops you can make your own. Spread molasses on strips of bright yellow poster board. Hang these strips in doorways any-where you find flies. You can also make squares to place on surfaces.

## COCKROACHES I

Cockroaches are deterred by the smell of eucalyptus or rosemary oils. Put a few drops of either oil onto cloth and place where you have cockroches. Refresh the oil every other day. Alternatively, mix 2 tablespoons of flour, 2 tablespoons of cocoa powder, and 4 tablespoons of borax and place the mixture in containers near the cockroaches.

## COCKROACHES II

You can make a trap for cockroaches by putting an overripe banana and half a bottle of beer into a glass jar. Rub the inside of the lid thick with petroleum jelly and tilt the jar for easy access for the cockroaches. Once inside, they will have difficulty in getting out.

## COCKROACHES III---ARE WE DONE YET?

Nothing is more revolting than roaches, except perhaps the chemicals we use to kill them. Try this instead: Make a mixture of equal parts cornstarch and plaster of Paris, and sprinkle it in the cracks where roaches appear. Then stand back, happily, and watch them croak.

## TOOTHPASTE, AGAIN?

Mice hate mint. If you can see the mice holes, smear a bit of mint toothpaste nearby and the smell will deter them.

## FLIES

Flies do not like the smell of lavender or cedar oil. Try using these oils with water in aromatherapy burners around your home so that the smell floats from room to room. Alternatively, try putting bowls of orange or lemon peel mixed with cloves around the house to keep flies at bay.

## DETER FLIES

Make sure garbage containers are tightly covered to avoid flies being drawn in. Circulate air in the house using fans as this also deters flies and keep fly swatters handy, a better alternative to using chemicals.

## MICE

Make sure any ways in for mice are sealed and stuff insulation around plumbing. If you want to avoid live traps, you can buy humane, chemical-free sonic devices that emit high-frequency waves to scare off rodents.

# CHIVES

Aphids hate chives, so they're a great choice to plant alongside your roses to help keep the pests away. If your roses are already suffering from aphids, pick them off by hand instead of using pesticide. Remember to wear gloves to protect your fingers from the thorns.

## FRUIT FLIES

For a natural way to trap annoying fruit flies, pour a small amount of beer into a wide-mouthed jar to attract them. Use a rubber band to secure a plastic bag across the mouth of the jar and poke a small hole in the bag. Flies will enter through the hole and not be able to find their way out again.

## MORE ABOUT FRUIT FLIES

Eliminate fruit flies the natural way: fill a spray bottle with water and rubbing alcohol, and spray away. It's about as effective as an insecticide, and you won't poison your family!

## PYRETHRUM DUST

Pyrethrum dust, which is made from chrysanthemums, will kill your unwanted aphids but it can also damage some susceptible plants and cause damage to other, beneficial insects so always use it with care. Pyrethrum dust is also the most environmentally-friendly option if you have a major caterpillar or slug problem and need to use chemicals because it kills the lower species but isn't passed up the food chain.

## SAY YES TO BIRDS AND NO TO MOSQUITOES

If you want to keep your bird bath full but is discourage mosquitoes from laying there eggs in the water, fear not: Simply add a few drops of vegetable oil to the water and the mosquitoes will go elsewhere.

## PINCH AWAY PESTS

The best way to remove pests from plants is to pinch them off with your fingers. You'll be sure they'll never come back without having to resort to poisons. To give the local wildlife a helping hand, make it a rule of thumb not to use pesticides or fertilizers in your garden. Even small amounts can build up in the food chain and cause harm to birds and mammals.

## DEATHLY DETERRENT

According to garden mythology, the best way to remove the pests from your garden is to collect slugs and create a liquid of their dead remains, by allowing it to decompose in natural rainwater for a few weeks. Then use the liquid around plants to protect them.

# SALT SLUGS

Although slugs are undesirable, birds and other wildlife might eat up to ten slugs a day, so the toxins in slug bait may build up and be harmful to them. Remove slugs by hand, or use salt pellets, which are wildlife friendly.

# SAWDUST SOLUTION

Stop slugs and snails from munching their way through your favorite plants with sawdust. It dries them out, effectively paralyzing them by preventing them from creating their slimy trail, which allows them to move.

## SQUIRT WITH SOAP

Use a squirt of mild soapy water to kill aphids and greenfly on roses and other garden plants. This simple solution prevents them from flying and subsequently suffocates them.

## START OFF INSIDE

Instead of protecting tender plants such as cucumber with chemical sprays outside, start them off inside where you can keep an eye on them until they are hardy enough to withstand the pests lurking outside.

## AND IF YOU DON'T HAVE SAWDUST?

Slugs are slimy. If you litter the ground surrounding your plants with gritty substances, slugs will not cross over it—it would be like you or I trying to crawl over broken glass. Use crushed eggshells, pine needles, sand—anything like that. Just be certain that the substance you choose will not harm the plants you are using it near.

## WORM AWAY SLUGS

If you have a slug problem but don't want to cover your garden with poisonous slug pellets, why not try natural methods instead? Buy a packet of nematodes. These are small worms that naturally parasitize the slugs and won't harm the rest of your garden.

## YOUR BIGGEST FAN

Don't let flying bugs ruin your backyard barbeque. Just turn on a few portable fans and aim it at the center of the party, where your guests are. It works great and the party won't stink of bug spray.

## CREATE A POND

If you have space, creating a pond or water feature in your garden is one of the best steps you can take to promote wildlife. Encouraging frogs and toads will mean you don't have to use slug bait, as they'll feast on your garden pests.

Who Knew?

Slugs are hermaphrodites: they all have male and female reproductive systems, so they can mate with themselves. They can also stretch to 20 times their normal length, enabling them to squeeze through openings to get at food. How revolting.

# PLANT DEFENSE

The problem with pesticides is that they are toxic to desirable wildlife as well as those you're trying to get rid of. Also, they enter the food, air, earth, and water systems so we consume them without being aware of the implications. Plant French marigolds throughout your garden—they work particularly well against tomato pests.

## THE EARLY BIRD CATCHES THE BUG

Birds are much more efficient than people at killing bugs, so for pest control, encourage birds into your garden with a birdhouse or birdfeeder. Finches, jays, robins, sparrows, cedar waxwings, starlings, and many other birds will consume thousands of insects every day.

## PLANT COMPANIONS

To encourage natural predators to munch away your garden pests so you don't have to use pesticide, consult your local garden society about local companion planting. The idea is that most plants have favorite "neighbors" that help to prevent disease.

## Who Knew?

According the National Wildlife Federation, there are almost 200 million spaces along our city streets where trees could be planted. This translates to the potential to absorb 33 million more tons of $CO_2$ every year—and would save about $4 billion a year in energy costs.

## SULFUR DUST

Sulfur (in dust or liquid form) controls mildew on roses and other flowers and vegetables, and although it's safe for animals, it can be fatally poisonous to fish, so be very careful when using it around water.

## KEEP 'EM GUESSING

One of the benefits of changing your garden each year is it helps prevent disease and pest infestation. If you never change the layout of your garden, it allows certain pests and diseases to settle in, and you don't want that.

# CHAMOMILE FOR FLIES

The smell of chamomile deters most small flies. Make your own natural pesticide by infusing chamomile flowers in hot water for 10 minutes. Spray on plants to kill pests.

# PLANT ONIONS

To stop harmful insects taking hold in your pesticide-free garden, plant onion plants, which will deter them from reproducing.

## BIRD HAVEN

Some plant species are known to attract birds into your garden and so reduce pests: pincherry, white flowering dogwood, honeysuckle, holly, white pine, Russian olive, sunflowers, and marigolds are all good choices.

## NET SEEDLINGS

Fine netting such as cheesecloth placed over flower and vegetable beds will protect seedlings from chewing insects, keep cats and birds away, and prevent flying insects from laying eggs. Create simple bamboo frames for the fabric to be attached to.

## GROW GARLIC

Growing garlic near your roses is a great way to protect them from aphids, as they can't bear the smell of garlic and won't come anywhere near your flowers.

## LOW TOXIC SOAP

For a chemical pest remover with low toxicity, try insecticidal soap. It can be bought from most hardware stores, and helps remove pests without leaving toxic resins on plants.

## FOR SQUIRRELS WHO STEAL

To keep squirrels from stealing from your bird feeder, just add a few teaspoons of cayenne pepper to your birdseed. The birds like it hot, the squirrels don't and your problem is solved.

# DETER CATS NATURALLY

Commercial cat deterrents may be harmful to garden birds. But since cats don't like the smell of citrus, instead you can just use essential oil repellents, which are totally natural. Try a few drops of lemon or orange essential oil in a spray bottle of water.

# PRICKLY SUBJECT

To deter ground mammals such as rabbits around your tender spring crops, sprinkle dried holly leaves, as the spikes will hurt their feet and discourage them from approaching. The leaves will biodegrade over time.

## DIATOMACEOUS EARTH

Diatomaceous earth (also known as DE, diatomite, or diahydro) is made from marine algae and can be found in garden centers. It consists of fossilized remains of diatoms, a type of hard-shelled algae. You can prevent slugs and snails eating leaves by sprinkling a ring of the earth around affected plants, as the earth dehydrates them. It is a dangerous dust and should be used with care, and not inhaled. Make sure it's not the crystalline or chemically manufactured variety you're buying.

## COMPOST HEAP

To keep your compost heap fresh and keep insects at bay, try adding lemon peel and basil, both of which are smells that flies and other insects hate. It will make the heap smell sweeter to your nose as well! If ants are a problem in your compost, it's a sign that it is too dry. Water it thoroughly, or, if some parts are wetter than others, give it a good turn.

## DON'T WORRY, JUST COMPOST

There are literally hundreds of books on the market devoted to composting, and achieving the correct carbon-to-nitrogen ratios. You don't need them. Composting is not that hard. Just remember that all organic material will compost in time...and pick up a novel instead.

## PROTECT YOUR CABBAGES

Try planting dill close to your cabbages, broccoli, and cauliflowers. It will keep cabbage worms under control by attracting wasps to keep pests under control. Alternatively, planting thyme around cabbage plants will deter cabbage worms, butterflies, and maggots.

## CUCUMBERS

Planting colorful nasturtiums close by can repel cucumber beetles. Their broad leaves should spread among the cucumber vines and create shelter for spiders, which will eat pests.

## THE COMBO PLATTER

A couple of facts to remember when planning your garden: shallow rooted plants thrive near deep-rooted plants, because they loosen the soil, providing drainage for the shallow rooted plants. Also, tall plants provide shade for smaller plants.

# TOMATOES

Basil not only goes well with tomato in cooking but also in your garden. Plant basil around tomato plants and it will help repel tomato hornworms.

# ZINNIAS ATTRACT LADYBUGS

Ladybugs eat pests such as aphids so attract these to your garden by planting zinnias. Plant zinnias around plants affected by aphids such as leafy greens.

## MARIGOLDS

Plant marigolds in your vegetable garden to help repel all manner of pests. The strong scent of the flower signals its repelling power. French marigolds help keep nematodes away from plants.

## ATTRACT GOOD INSECTS

Pollinating insects are beneficial to fruit trees and fruiting vegetables such as squashes. Attract these to your garden by mixing the following spray. Boil ¼ of a cup of sugar in 1 cup of water until it dissolves then allow to cool. Pour into a spray bottle and add 2 quarts of water. Spray this solution in your garden to attract pollinating insects.

## FOR A GARDEN IN A HURRY

Sunflowers are one of the fastest growing plants, and can grow 8 to 12 feet tall in rich soil within six months. If you need some height in your garden in a hurry, take note.

 Who Knew?

White flowers tend to be more strongly scented than flowers of other colors.

## SOAP SPRAY

Kill spider mites, aphids, and whiteflies by mixing together 1 tablespoon of natural dishwashing soap with 2 quarts of water in a spray bottle. Shake well, then spray liberally on affected plants every week and after it has rained until the pests have gone. It is best to spray plants in the evening or on cloudy days rather than in the full sun.

## MILKY SPORE TO THE RESCUE

Milky spore is a natural remedy to rid your lawn or garden of grubs. It works by causing the grubs to contract a disease that kills them, but it leaves the beneficial organisms unharmed. Milky spore multiplies over time and will sit inactive, waiting for grubs to infect.

# PEST PATROL

Check plants once a week for pests. The most environmentally friendly way to remove slugs and snails is to pick them off by hand. Smaller pests can be washed off plants with a spray of water. Alternatively try some of the natural spray solutions given here. Always test a new spray on a few plants before using on your whole garden as even natural sprays can harm delicate leaves.

## GARLIC AND PEPPER SPRAY

Here is another way to prevent insects from eating your plants.

    5 cloves garlic

    8 jalapeno peppers

    ½ teaspoon natural dishwashing soap

    water

Chop the garlic and jalapeno peppers, and add to 1 quart of water. Leave overnight, then strain, and put liquid in a spray bottle. Add the natural dishwashing soap and shake well. Spray plants once a week and after rain until pests have gone.

## SAY GOODBYE TO APHIDS, MEALYBUGS AND MITES

All soft-bodied insects are repelled by this simple formula: combine one tablespoon canola oil with a few drops of natural dishwashing soap in a quart of water. Shake well and pour into a spray bottle. Spray plant carefully, making sure you get the underside of the leaves. The oil smothers the insects.

## FUNGAL DISEASE SPRAY

You can rid your garden of fungal diseases by combining one tablespoon of cooking oil, two table-spoons of baking soda and a few drops of natural dishwashing soap into a quart of water. Pour into a spray container and both sides of the leaves.

## WORMWOOD SPRAY

Keep aphids at bay with this wormwood tea spray.

    2 cups of chopped fresh wormwood leaves

    water

    ½ teaspoon natural dishwashing soap

Put the fresh wormwood leaves in a bowl and pour over 1 quart of boiling water and leave to cool. Strain and pour into a spray bottle before adding the natural dishwashing soap. Shake well and spray on plants.

## POTATO SPRAY

This potato spray is non-toxic but suffocates pests such as aphids and whiteflies.

    ¼ cup of potato flour

    1 teaspoon natural dishwashing soap

    Water

Mix the potato flour with 1 quart of warm water until dissolved. Pour into a spray bottle and add the natural dishwashing soap. Shake well and spray on plants.

# ESSENTIAL OIL SPRAY

This combination of lavender, sage, and thyme helps control garden pests.

    thyme oil

    sage oil

    lavender oil

    1 teaspoon of vodka.

    water

Mix 3 drops of thyme oil, 3 drops of sage oil, and 5 drops of lavender oil with the vodka. Add 2 quarts of water and pour into a spray bottle, shake well, spray liberally on your plants.

# TOMATO SPRAY

Tomato leaves are toxic because they are rich in alkaloids. That's what makes this formula so effective at killing aphids and corn earworms.

- 2 cups chopped tomato leaves
- 1 teaspoon natural dishwashing soap
- water

Soak the chopped tomato leaves overnight in 1 quart of water. Strain and pour into a spray bottle. Add the natural dishwashing soap, shake well, and spray on plants.

## TOBACCO SPRAY

Nicotine is highly toxic not only to pests such as aphids but also to good insects so use only as a last resort.

- ½ cup of dried, crushed tobacco leaves
- 1 teaspoon natural dishwashing soap
- water

Soak the tobacco leaves in 2 quarts of warm water for half an hour then strain the liquid into a spray bottle. Add the natural dishwashing soap and shake well before spraying leaves with the solution. Remember, nicotine is poisonous to humans too so take care when using.

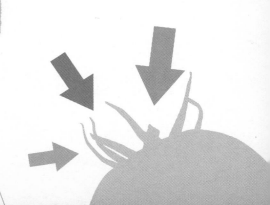

## HOT PEPPER DUST

This spicy combination will help repel ants from plants in your garden. Mix ½ a cup each of powdered cayenne pepper, powdered garlic, and powdered dill and sprinkle liberally around plants. If you cannot buy the powdered forms, then grind up dried herbs in a coffee grinder.

## SLUGS AND SNAILS

Sprinkling salt on slugs will dehydrate them. You can also create humane traps by leaving upturned flowerpots out overnight as they will often crawl in, and you will be able to remove them in the morning.

## PAPER TRICKS

Cut a slit in the middle of a 6-inch square of stiff paper and place carefully around the base of your young cabbage plants when planting. This will deter cabbage root flies that lay their eggs at the base of the plant. The maggots that hatch from the eggs then burrow into the roots and kill the plants.

## BEER TRAP

Slugs and snails also like stale beer so bury a container of beer so that the top is level with the ground. Leave out overnight and the slugs and snails will be in the trap in the morning.

## COPPER DETERENTS

One way to repel slugs and snails without killing them is to use copper strips you can buy from garden centers. Generally these pests do not cross copper because it gives them a mild electric shock. Bury the strips partially into the ground and create an outward lip.

## KEEP YOUR CABBAGE HEALTHY

Caterpillars on cabbage plants can be treated with *Bacillus thuringiensis* (BT), which is a naturally occurring bacteria. BT kills caterpillars but is not toxic to humans or mammals, and it won't kill the larvae of other butterflies.

## CUTWORMS

Cutworms are fat gray or brown caterpillars that can devour your vegetable garden, especially small seedlings and young plant stems. Prevention is most effective here, so use cardboard rolls from toilet paper and paper towels, cut to size, to place around young plants to keep pests at bay. Push them 1 inch into the soil, and leave about 5 inches above. If you do have cutworms in your garden, make use of birds' taste for them by turning over your soil to expose them. The birds will get rid of many of them for you.

## WIREWORMS

Wireworms (the larvae of beetles) burrow into carrots and potatoes. To set a trap, try cutting pieces of potato and threading on a skewer. Push into the ground leaving some skewer above ground so you can find it again. After a few days you should find you have larvae in your trap and can dispose of them.

# MILDEW

Use this solution to removing white or gray mildew coating from leaves.

- 1 teaspoon light vegetable oil
- tea tree oil
- 1 teaspoon baking soda
- water

Mix together vegetable oil, 10 drops of tea tree oil, baking soda, and 1 gallon of water. Shake well and decant into a spray bottle. After washing off the affected leaves, spray on the solution once a week.

## EARWIGS (NIGHT)

Earwigs are those disgusting roach-like bugs with the pinchers on them, which we all hate. They are attracted to soft plants such as lettuce at nighttime. You can trap them by filling an unwashed tuna can with ½ an inch of vegetable oil and 1 teaspoon of molasses. Place traps near affected plants.

## EARWIGS (DAY)

In the daytime, earwigs look for dark moist places to hide. Moisten newspaper with water and roll up and secure will an elastic band. Place a few around your garden and you should find the earwigs are attracted to them.

## SOLAR POWER

Raising the soil temperature eradicates pests and disease but only use this method as a last resort as it also kills beneficial organisms. You can use the power of the sun to solarize soil by removing all plants and weeds, cultivate and rake the soil, then water it. Dig a trench 6 inches deep around the edge of the bed. Cover the soil in the bed with a plastic sheet and tuck the ends into the trench and fill with soil. Leave for 2 months. When you remove the plastic add compost to your soil to help restore the good organisms.

## BLOSSOM END ROT

Blossom end rot is a troublesome disease, familiar to most gardeners who have grown tomatoes. This disease is seen on tomatoes, peppers, and others when a dark sunken area is seen at the blossom end. Caused by calcium deficiency or uneven watering, it can be remedied by adding bone meal to beds or by adding 2 tablespoons of Epsom salts in planting holes, and by making sure plants are getting 1 inch of water a week. Also mulch plants to keep the soil moist.

## EPSOM SALTS FOR ROSES

Epsom salts are also useful for roses. The magnesium helps rose plants absorb nutrients, giving roses more blooms and better color. Sprinkle 1 teaspoon for every foot of plant height in springtime and repeat regularly until roses bloom.

## BLACK SPOT

This fungal disease often affects roses and will leave black spots surrounded by yellow rings on leaves. Prevention methods include not watering plants from overhead and adding fresh mulch every spring. If you have black spot, remove the affected leaves and mix together 1 tablespoon of baking soda, 1 teaspoon of natural dishwashing soap, and 1 gallon of warm water. Pour into a spray bottle and spray plants once a week.

# ONE MORE MOSQUITO TIP

Mosquitoes need water, primarily still or stagnant water rich in organic matter upon which mosquito larvae can feed. The saucers usually found under potted plants, especially on decks and patios, is a perfect breeding ground. One option is to remove the saucers altogether, or at least dump them every couple of days.

## CITRONELLA

When outside in hot weather, light a few citronella-scented candles to deter mosquitoes and other bugs. Place them in torches around the year to keep the area clear.

## WASPS

Unlike bees, wasps can sting again and again. For small numbers, fill a jar with half jam and half water. Cover with paper punctured with holes to attract, trap, and drown them. If you spot wasps flying to one spot, look for a nest. Wasp nests can produce up to 30,000 wasps. Contact the authorities to remove it without delay.

## AND FINALLY, KEEP IT LOCAL WHEN BUYING PLANTS

Buy local transplants to avoid bringing non-native unwanted insects into your garden. Add mulch and keep your garden in good shape. Healthy plants are naturally more resistant to predators.

# NOTES

# who knew?
## online

**Visit us on the web at WhoKnewTips.com!**

* Money-saving tips
* Quick 'n' easy recipes
* Who Knew? products
* And much more!

 Twitter.com/WhoKnewTips
Get a free daily tip and ask us your questions

 YouTube.com/WhoKnewTips
Watch demos of your favorite tips

 Facebook.com/WhoKnewTips
Daily tips, giveaways, and more fun!